Marxist Modernism

Marxist Modernism

Introductory Lectures on
Frankfurt School Critical Theory

Gillian Rose

Edited by Robert Lucas Scott and James Gordon Finlayson

VERSO
London · New York

First published by Verso 2024
Collection © Verso 2024
Editor's Introduction © Robert Lucas Scott and James Gordon Finlayson
Lectures © Literary Estate of Gillian Rose
Afterword © Martin Jay

The editors are grateful to Howard Caygill as Gillian Rose's literary
executor for the permission to publish these lectures.

3 5 7 9 10 8 6 4 2

Verso
UK: 6 Meard Street, London W1F 0EG
US: 388 Atlantic Avenue, Brooklyn, NY 11217
versobooks.com

Verso is the imprint of New Left Books

ISBN-13: 978-1-80429-011-8
ISBN-13: 978-1-80429-012-5 (UK EBK)
ISBN-13: 978-1-80429-013-2 (US EBK)

British Library Cataloguing in Publication Data
A catalogue record for this book is available from the British Library

Library of Congress Cataloging-in-Publication Data

Names: Rose, Gillian, author. | Scott, Robert Lucas, editor. | Finlayson,
  James Gordon, editor.
Title: Marxist modernism : introductory lectures on Frankfurt School
  Critical Theory / Gillian Rose ; edited by Robert Lucas Scott and James
  Gordon Finlayson.
Description: London ; New York : Verso, 2024. | Includes bibliographical
  references and index.
Identifiers: LCCN 2024003027 (print) | LCCN 2024003028 (ebook) | ISBN
  9781804290118 (trade paperback) | ISBN 9781804290132 (ebook)
Subjects: LCSH: Marxian school of sociology. | Marxian school of sociology.
Classification: LCC HM471 .R674 2024 (print) | LCC HM471 (ebook) | DDC
  301.01—dc23/eng/20240412
LC record available at https://lccn.loc.gov/2024003027
LC ebook record available at https://lccn.loc.gov/2024003028

FSC
www.fsc.org
MIX
Paper | Supporting
responsible forestry
FSC® C171272

Typeset in Minion by Hewer Text UK Ltd, Edinburgh
Printed and bound by CPI Group (UK) Ltd, Croydon CR0 4YY

Contents

Editors' Introduction: Gillian Rose and the Difficulty of Critical Theory
Robert Lucas Scott and James Gordon Finlayson

It is often remarked that Gillian Rose (1947–1995) is a difficult thinker. She certainly makes few concessions to her reader. Not only do her major works often engage with a prodigious range of disciplines and traditions – from philosophy to theology, legal theory, Judaica, literary modernism, political theory, sociology, even architecture – her style of writing is also variously esoteric, ironic, poetic, and characterised by an almost paradoxical tone of both levity and severity. *The Melancholy Science* (1978), her first book, claims to be *An Introduction to the Thought of Theodor W. Adorno*, but, as Howard Caygill comments, 'readers looking to be introduced were quickly dismayed.'[1] Her next book, *Hegel Contra Sociology* (1981), argues that recurrent issues in social theory and Marxism can be better approached via a close analysis of Hegel's critiques of Kant and Fichte, and a retrieval of his corresponding idea of 'speculative experience'. It is, in the judgement of Peter Osborne, 'unashamedly, and sadly, an extremely difficult book.'[2] *The Broken Middle: Out of Our Ancient*

---

1 Howard Caygill, 'Editor's Preface', in Gillian Rose, *Paradiso* (London: Shearsman, 1999), p. 7.
2 Peter Osborne, 'Hegelian Phenomenology and the Critique of Reason and Society', *Radical Philosophy* 32 (1982), p. 8.

Society (1992) – which contests the postmodern conception of philosophy as systematic and spuriously totalising – is perhaps her most difficult of all. Andrew Shanks describes the reading experience as like coming across 'an accumulation of marginal notes compiled originally for herself alone – abstruse musings, studded with arcane witticisms'.[3] Rose relishes and embraces difficulty, whether in the works she engages with – for example, Adorno's many 'aporia', a word that in Greek literally means dead-end or 'no path' – or the 'broken middle' in her own. As Jacqueline Rose succinctly puts it: 'Difficulty was one of her favourite words.'[4]

This commitment to difficulty is perhaps a major reason why her writing remains comparatively understudied by wider audiences. The present volume, however, comprises a series of introductory lectures that Rose delivered to undergraduates at the University of Sussex in 1979 on Frankfurt School Critical Theory. While they exhibit her commitment to the aporia of political and ethical life, they do so in a conversational and accessible pedagogic style. Deftly explaining the positions of Georg Lukács, Ernst Bloch, Walter Benjamin, Bertolt Brecht, Max Horkheimer, and Theodor Adorno, Rose provides a way into the difficulties they present. It is at once an introduction to Frankfurt School Critical Theory and also an introduction to the questions and concerns that would go on to animate her whole oeuvre.

Marxist Modernism could be read as something of a companion piece to Rose's first book, *The Melancholy Science*, published in the previous year, 1978.[5] One main argument of *The Melancholy Science*

---

3   Andrew Shanks, *Against Innocence: Gillian Rose and the Gift of Faith* (London: SCM, 2008), p. 48.

4   Jacqueline Rose, 'On Gillian Rose', in *The Last Resistance* (London: Verso, 2007), p. 224.

5   Rose would joke that this work 'began life as a commission to write a *cookery* book' (Caygill, 'Editor's Preface', p. 7). In fact, it was developed from her doctoral thesis entitled 'Reification as a Sociological Category: Theodor W. Adorno's Concept of Reification and the Possibility of a Critical Theory of Society', completed in 1976 at the University of Oxford under the supervision of the Polish philosopher Leszek Kołakowski. This is in spite of the fact that Kołakowski was highly suspicious of

is that the work of Adorno, though varied and fragmented, is all directed towards the development of a Marxist theory of culture centred on the concept of 'reification'. Lukács and Benjamin are shown to be engaged in this task too, but unlike Adorno, Rose argues, neither of them pursue the consequences of this theory to their end. *Marxist Modernism* extends this work by also bringing in the work of Brecht and Bloch, who only receive a passing reference in *The Melancholy Science*. While everything in *The Melancholy Science* is directed towards an understanding of Adorno's Marxist theory of culture, *Marxist Modernism* adopts a broader focus, exploring how other Marxist thinkers were concerned with this question at the time.

When Rose delivered these lectures, this was cutting-edge material for an Anglophone audience. Rose notes in a later lecture from 1986 (not included in this collection):

> When I first gave this lecture, which was longer ago than I like to remember, there was very little knowledge or teaching of Critical Theory or the Frankfurt School in this country. In fact, if I might say something personal, I was one of the first people who did doctoral research on this subject, and when I did it . . . I was the only person in the country working on this stuff. I was completely and utterly isolated.[6]

As grand as this claim may be, what is certain is that, over three decades later, Frankfurt School Critical Theory is commonly studied in sociology, cultural studies, philosophy, and intellectual history departments throughout the world.

What, then, is critical theory? The term has come to stand for any attempt to understand society and culture with reference to its

---

Adorno's value. 'I, too, wrote my thesis on a second-rate thinker', he is supposed to have said to her. (His thesis, incidentally, was on Spinoza.) 'Professor Gillian Rose; Obituary', *The Times*, 14 December 1995.

6   Gillian Rose, 'Introduction to Critical Theory' (unpublished lecture recording, University of Sussex, 1986).

underlying power structures. There is also usually the assumption for critical theorists that, by revealing these underlying power structures, one presents the opportunity for transgressing or overcoming them. By understanding the conditions of our unjust world, we might be able to reform or revolutionise them, and thus make a different world possible. An introductory lecture series on critical theory today might therefore cover everything from Marxism to poststructuralism, gender studies, critical race theory, Foucauldian discourse analysis, psychoanalysis, queer theory, postcolonialism, and ecocriticism.

For Rose, the term 'Critical Theory' has a narrower meaning.[7] It refers principally to the work of several German philosophers and social theorists who came to be known collectively as the Frankfurt School, and who were associated with the Institute for Social Research (founded in 1929–1930) in Frankfurt. It also refers to some contemporary thinkers who were never 'members', but worked closely with them – principally Ernst Bloch, Walter Benjamin, and Bertolt Brecht. Rose locates Critical Theory's origin, however, a decade earlier, in the seminal work of the germanophone Hungarian philosopher Georg Lukács and his critique of what he took to be the vulgar Marxism of the socialist and communist parties of Europe. Lukács lamented that Marxism had become, in Rose's words, 'passive, deterministic, and descriptive' (p. 7 of this collection). It had become too formulaic, always falling back on stock answers rather than engaging in difficult concrete analysis. Instead, he argued, it was necessary to emphasise the complex and varied configurations of economic conditions, on the one hand, and human subjectivity and consciousness, on the other. One cannot talk only about abstract economic laws of exchange and production; one must grasp how they are concretely realised, and how they are subjectively experienced and mediated. In other words, while Marxism had become a mechanistic theory concerning the iron laws of history and class struggle, with an established doctrine

---

7   The capitals on 'Critical Theory' indicate that we use it as the name for the approach of the Frankfurt School, rather than for anything more capacious and general.

and cache of slogans, it had done so at the expense of grasping reality or society as 'human sensuous activity, as practice, subjectively' (as Rose quotes from Marx's 'Theses on Feuerbach').

Critical Theory as Rose construes it, then, arises from a critique of Marxism – though this does not mean it abandons Marxism (indeed, Rose uses the terms 'Critical Theory' and 'critical Marxism' interchangeably). Rather, Critical Theory, for Rose, is the name for a more open and dialectical view of Marxism. As she puts it in a later essay, critical Marxism should be conceived as

> stressing the gap between theory and practice, which strain towards each other; as insisting on the uncertain course of class struggle, which depends on the unpredictable configurations of objective conditions and the formation of class consciousness; as imagining the multiplicity of eventualities which might emerge between the extremes, 'Barbarism or Socialism'.[8]

Thus, for Rose, Critical Theory is the labour of making Marxism difficult again.

The necessity for this new form of difficult Marxism was particularly pressing for Frankfurt School Critical Theorists (as it was for Rose), since twentieth-century Marxists found themselves in a situation in which no easy or clear solutions presented themselves. Despite the explanatory power of Marxism, its practical realisation had not been successful. In the West, the revolutionary subject did not emerge, or was defeated, while capitalism was consolidated and expanded; while in the East, revolutionary change had reverted into old forms of hierarchy, totalitarianism, and domination. The questions posed by Lukács in *History and Class Consciousness* (1923) later taken up by all the Frankfurt School theorists were these: What had made capitalism so resistant to revolutionary change? What had doused the revolutionary fire? And what prevents the embers from being rekindled?

---

8 Gillian Rose, *Mourning Becomes the Law: Philosophy and Representation* (Cambridge: Cambridge University Press, 1996), p. 8.

Rose argues that, for Lukács and the Critical Theorists, all of these questions have a single answer: 'commodity fetishism'. Commodity fetishism is the principal stumbling block of capitalism, which has enabled it to thwart all attempts at overcoming it. True, each of the Critical Theorists develops different accounts of commodity fetishism and what may or may not be done about it. Nevertheless, Rose argues, all of them view the idea as centrally important. This is why Rose (after Adorno) refers to the *possibility* of a Critical Theory. What if there is something inherent to capitalism – that is, commodity fetishism – that means we simply cannot easily comprehend or critically theorise it, that it is essentially liable to be misunderstood?

Rose's answer to the question 'What is Critical Theory?' begins from the question 'What is commodity fetishism?' Commodity fetishism – or, perhaps more properly, 'the fetish character of the commodity' (*der Fetischcharakter der Ware*, in the original German) – is Marx's term for a feature inherent to all commodities that prevents us from grasping their essence. Marx argues in *Capital* that there is something about commodities and the way in which they are produced and exchanged under capitalism that hides their historical and socially mediated significance beneath an appearance or sheen (in German, *Schein*) of naturalness, or matter-of-factness.[9] Of course, a commodity *is* a good that satisfies some need (what Marx called its 'use' value). But it is *also* a product that can be bought and sold for profit. Where does this profit come from? This, according to Marx, is the 'secret' that the commodity hides. What is hidden by the commodity fetish is the fact that what determines this value is *labour*. 'The value of a commodity is the quantity of simple labour . . . socially necessary for its production.'[10] In Rose's words: 'People think that value inheres in the product itself, and they do not understand that in fact it is the expression of specific social relations and activities between people' (p. 16). The ultimate source of value is the socially

9   *Schein* in German means both surface appearance and illusion.
10   Karl Marx, *Capital: A Critique of Political Economy*, vol. 1, transl. Ben Fowkes (London: Penguin, 1976), p. 38.

necessary labour time invested in the production of the commodity, which the worker sells to the capitalist.

According to Marx, we fetishise a commodity – and we cannot but fetishise it when we are engaged in the practice of commodity exchange – when we treat its value as a property inherent in it, 'when in fact,' as Rose puts it, 'it is the expression of determinate social relations between people' (p. 16). Crucially, simply knowing about this fetish character is not enough to overcome the illusion, for the illusion inheres in commodities themselves, and in the reality of capitalist commodity exchange. In this, it is somewhat like the illusion that the Sun orbits the Earth, which is difficult to shake off even when we know that the opposite is the case: the knowledge alone does not alter the illusion-generating mechanism. As Rose notes: 'Marx is not saying, for example, that the illusions that arise out of commodity fetishism are wrong; he is saying that those illusions are necessary and real, but nevertheless, they are illusions' (p. 17). When it comes to commodities, the illusion-generating mechanism is the particular relation of production that consists in the fact that labourers have nothing to sell but their labour time, which they are forced to sell in exchange for wages – while the capitalist keeps the product and all the 'surplus value' generated by its production and sale. We think of capitalism as a relationship between things – the market, the economy, supply and demand – but in reality it is an exploitative and destructive relationship between human beings that is marked by the domination of one class by another. This dialectic between the illusion and its reality, then, cannot be undone by an act of analysis, for the illusion is a necessary and unavoidable product of that reality. It is the reality itself, along with the illusion-generating mechanism, that has to be revolutionised if the illusion is to be fully dispelled.

Rose's overarching thesis in these lectures is that the central move of Critical Theory is to generalise and radicalise Marx's theory of commodity fetishism to cover all areas of society, producing a new theory of what they called 'reification'. This was the seminal and ingenious move that Lukács made in *History and Class Consciousness*. He first assumed that the commodity form posed not just the central problem in economics, but the 'central, structural problem of capitalist society in all its aspects'.[11] Fetishism was a virtually universal phenomenon, or group of diverse but related phenomena, affecting the domains of bourgeois economics, law, culture, and all forms of thought, including philosophy. 'Reification' – from the Latin *res*, meaning 'being' or 'thing' – refers to the act of taking something abstract to be a physical thing. Its effect is to disguise the history and the socially determined nature of something (for example, a commodity) so that it appears to be a natural or factual phenomenon, which human beings merely contemplate theoretically or adapt to practically. The counterpart to 'reification' is what Lukács calls 'the contemplative attitude': 'mere contemplation and mere intuition' become the dominant modes of perception and thought under bourgeois capitalist conditions.[12] This false or illusory naturalisation of things that are in reality historically and socially determined leads swiftly to human beings' becoming blind to and disconnected from their historical significance and social agency. The social world that is in fact up to us, in that it is historically contingent and in principle alterable, seems to us to be otherwise. Economic laws, for example, have the allure of being fixed, necessary, and independent of human thought and action. Ultimately, then, the various kinds of reification and their effects lead to alienation of human beings from their own powers, allowing them to be dominated and oppressed by a social and economic system that should serve their deepest interests, but in reality thwarts them.[13]

While Lukács had fraught relations with the communist parties in Hungary and the Soviet Union, he was nonetheless a committed

---

11   Georg Lukács, *History and Class Consciousness: Studies in Marxist Dialectics*, transl. Rodney Livingston (London: Merlin, 2010), p. 83.

12   Ibid., p. 122.

13   Lukács's genius here was to anticipate Marx's theory of alienation in the *Economic and Philosophical Manuscripts* four years before their discovery in Paris in 1927. Incidentally, the Frankfurt School theorist Herbert Marcuse was among the first to review these 1844 works. He argued that their publication was 'a crucial event in the history of Marxist studies', and that they should reorient debates about the theories of historical materialism and 'scientific socialism', and about Marx's relation to Hegel. See Herbert Marcuse, 'The Foundation of Historical Materialism (1932)', *Studies in Critical Philosophy*, transl. Joris de Bres (Boston: Beacon, 1972), p. 3.

communist and revolutionary. He thought that the still glowing embers of socialist revolution could be rekindled, provided the proletariat could be brought to class-consciousness and constitute itself as the subject and object of history. The peculiar 'standpoint' of the proletariat, as both fully subject – the source of human labour and all value – and fully object – insofar as its labour power was bought and sold on the market like any other commodity – would allow it to break free from the theoretical and practical hold of reification. 'History is at its least automatic when it is the consciousness of the proletariat that is at issue. The truth that the old intuitive, mechanistic materialism could not grasp turns out to be . . . that [the proletariat] can be transformed and liberated only by its own actions.'[14]

However much inspiration the Frankfurt School Critical Theorists drew from Lukács in their own diagnosis of the time and in their own methods, they did not ultimately share his view that communism was the immediate answer to the problem of capitalism, or his optimism about the prospects for revolutionary transformation. In his seminal 1937 essay 'Traditional and Critical Theory', Max Horkheimer argued, for example, that 'the situation of the proletariat is, in this society, no guarantee of correct knowledge.'[15] They believed in the theory of reification, but argued that no one – not even the proletariat, the putative subject and object of history – was immune from its illusory hold: 'Even to the proletariat the world superficially seems quite different than it really is.'[16]

This is the crucial and, some would argue, fateful step towards an 'aporetic' Marxism of the kind that Adorno, and subsequently also Rose, would embrace. In Adorno, what one can call 'utopophobia' takes a radical turn. He believed that, under the present conditions, it was impossible to even imagine what a better world would look like. The reasons for this run deep in his theory. They flow, on the one hand, from his negativism and the methodological significance he

---

14   Lukács, *History and Class Consciousness*, p. 208.

15   Max Horkheimer, 'Traditional and Critical Theory', transl. Matthew J. O'Connell, *Critical Theory: Selected Essays* (New York: Continuum, 1972), p. 213.

16   Ibid., p. 214.

attaches to the 'ban on images', and, on the other, from his political hesitancy and worries about paternalism and incipient forms of authoritarianism among the student radicals. The practical dimension of Adorno's aporetic Marxism takes the following paradoxical form: only a revolution will do; but no revolution is near, where revolution is understood as radical qualitative social change for the better, rather than as violent class insurrection. It is true that almost all of Adorno's philosophy radiates in one direction or other from this central aporia: whether it is in 'open thinking' that 'points beyond itself'; the motif of attempting to see the world 'from the standpoint of redemption . . . as indigent and distorted as it will appear one day in the messianic light'; or the attempt to experience the '*promesse du bonheur*' that shines from certain works of avant-garde art, and to decode the riddles of mute artworks by means of a philosophy of non-identity whose insights remain ultimately ineffable.[17] To what extent such motifs actually represent a way out of the aporia, or merely throw some new light on it, is a matter of ongoing debate.

The aporia at the heart of Adorno's Marxism creates a number of obvious difficulties, notably of how to connect Marxist theory to any meaningful political practice. But it does explain why the Frankfurt School, and also Rose in these lectures and elsewhere, were so preoccupied with culture, and cultural movements like expressionism and modernism. While Marxists had traditionally conceived of domination primarily in terms of economics and politics, Lukács and even more so Adorno are concerned with art, literature, and music both as a means of oppression and ideological mystification, and as a means of possible resistance – a means of

---

17   Theodor W. Adorno, 'Resignation', in *Critical Models: Interventions and Catchwords*, transl. Henry W. Pickford (New York: Columbia University Press, 1998), p. 293; Theodor W. Adorno, *Minima Moralia: Reflections on a Damaged Life*, transl. E. F. N. Jephcott (London: Verso, 2005), p. 247. The phrase 'promesse du bonheur' and related expressions occur many times in Adorno's work, but see especially Theodor W. Adorno, *Aesthetic Theory*, transl. R. Hullot-Kentor (London: Athlone Press, 1999), pp. 12 and 311. See also James Gordon Finlayson, 'The Artwork and the *Promesse du Bonheur* in Adorno', *European Journal of Philosophy* 23: 3 (2015), pp. 392–419.

reinforcing reification, or undermining it. More generally, the new Marxism led the Frankfurt School to 'stress the subjective correlates of reification – that is, how people experience it, how it prevents people from understanding society, and the social forces which are structuring their lives' (p. 33). To illustrate this, Rose reformulates the second-wave feminist slogan 'The personal is political.' For the Frankfurt School, 'The *cultural* had become political' (p. 8). This is what connects them so closely intellectually to their contemporaries Brecht and Benjamin, what directs their attention to the popular and avant-garde cultures of their day (such as Thomas Mann, Samuel Beckett, Arnold Schoenberg, jazz, and Hollywood), and what, ultimately, leads them to interrogate the political effect and critical efficacy of various forms of modernism and realism. Rose also stresses, for this same reason, that some Critical Theorists were artists. Most notably, Walter Benjamin was a short story writer, Bertolt Brecht a poet and playwright, and Adorno a composer and accomplished pianist.[18]

Lukács's diagnosis of the time had already called into question the orthodox model of understanding society in terms of an economic 'base' and an ideological 'superstructure', the idea that the forces and relations of commodity production (the base) shapes all other relations – culture, religion, media, the state, law, roles, rituals, and so on (the superstructure) – which in turn maintain the forces and relations of production. This base–superstructure model, in Rose's words, 'reduce[s] institutional and ideological formations to mere epiphenomena or to simple reflections of a base' (p. 17). A model based on reification, by contrast, 'would provide a sociological explanation for the social determination yet relative autonomy of other social forms, such as culture. It provided a way of saying that something is both socially determined and yet also partially autonomous.' This new model focused on the various social and psychological mechanisms of the pacification of class struggle, brought the diagnostic task of

---

18   Rose also incorrectly says that Ernst Bloch was a composer, presumably confusing him with the American composer Ernest Bloch. See Martin Jay's afterword, p. 133. Ernst Bloch did, however, write widely on music and musicology.

critical theory to the fore, and deferred practical and political aims into an indefinite future.

The course at the University of Sussex for which Rose composed this lecture series, 'Modern European Mind', was usually divided into two parts: 'Diagnosis' and 'Expression' – thinkers who diagnose modernity, and writers who express it. From the start, however, Rose insists that 'it is quite impossible to maintain these distinctions, between diagnosis and expression, or ideas and literature' (p. 5). It is fundamental, for Rose, that the two go hand in hand, and that the distinction between them is blurred. This accounts for the title of this volume (Rose's title for the lecture series was in fact just 'The Frankfurt School'). In her own words:

> Art like Marxism, Marxism like art, must modernise itself if it was to continue to have any importance in face of colossal political and social change. They – that is, Critical Theorists – differed, and they differed often bitterly, over how this modernisation should be achieved. But they all applied their principles of innovation to both their theoretical and their artistic work. (p. 9)

It is for this reason that the Critical Theorists – and in particular Adorno, Bloch, Brecht, and Benjamin – were preoccupied with the question of style, and experimented widely with the presentation of their own work, a topic to which Rose dedicates great attention in her lectures. To what extent does the style of a philosophy contribute to its substance? To what extent can the two be separated? Can a new style produce a new thought? Can a particular style – for example, a self-consciously difficult and aporetic style – loosen the shackles of reification, or at least make the presence and experience of reification more apparent? The focus in this volume on these questions as they relate to the Frankfurt School is particularly interesting for readers of Rose, as style would go on to be a central concern of her own work, both thematically and practically, as she experimented variously with what she called the 'severe' and 'facetious' styles, essays, memoir, and even verse. However, as we noted earlier, Rose's lectures on Marxist modernism, not unlike Adorno's lectures in this respect, are more informal and conversational, tailored to the pedagogic goals of teaching and education. In these lectures, style and form take a back seat to the practical goal of inviting students in to encounter the difficulties of the thinkers under discussion, and hopefully 'leading them out' again (which is the etymological meaning of the verb 'to educate'), not into the light of day, but into a deeper understanding of its darkness.[19]

19   On the trope of obscurity in Adorno see James Gordon Finlayson, 'On Not Being Silent in the Darkness: Adorno's Singular Apophaticism', *Harvard Theological Review* 105: 1 (2012), pp. 1–37, and Adorno's essay 'Skoteinos' in his *Hegel Three Studies*, transl. Shierry Weber Nicholsen (Cambridge, MA: MIT Press, 1993), pp. 89–149.

Marxist Modernism

1

Introduction: Marxist Modernism

Although the title of this lecture series is 'The Frankfurt School', it is intended for students reading 'Modern European Mind'.[1] I would be quite interested to know how many of the people here are *not* in fact reading Modern European Mind . . . Oh, I think it's the majority. Okay, that's very interesting. Some of you are, presumably. I stress this because obviously it's not the same as a general lecture series on the Frankfurt School. I have organised this lecture series to bring out the

---

1 The 'Modern European Mind' course originated in the School of English Studies at the University of Sussex in 1961, but was soon shared with the School of European Studies. The literary critic David Daiches, who founded the English department at Sussex, describes the rationale for the course as follows: 'We have chosen to investigate the response of the literary imagination to the world of modern industrial democracy, from the mid-nineteenth century to the present . . . We have chosen this because of the enormous historical importance of this response and also because so many of the students' own preconceptions about art and its relation to life will have been conditioned by it, without being aware of it. Many of what the students will consider the simplest truths about the relation of the artist to his environment are in fact the product of this special modern institution.' In her lecture series, Rose assumes this rationale with a particular focus on the aesthetic debates of the Frankfurt School. David Daiches, 'The Place of English Studies in the Sussex Scheme', in David Daiches, ed., *The Idea of a New University: An Experiment in Sussex* (London: André Deutsch, 1964), p. 92.

connections between the Frankfurt School and the things that people are concerned with on the course Modern European Mind, so those of you not reading Modern European Mind should bear that in mind, that this is not a general lecture course on the Frankfurt School. I hope to speak for forty to fifty minutes and leave some time for discussion, or for you to come and ask questions individually if you want to, so don't be hesitant in doing that. Let me know, as well, if I speak too slowly or too fast, or if you find the material too difficult or too easy.

Today's introductory lecture, which is called 'Marxist Modernism', will be divided into two halves. In the first half I shall try and explain why a lecture series on the Frankfurt School is relevant to the course Modern European Mind, and I shall do this by examining some of the different rationales for Modern European Mind. I shall then try and show how a discussion of the Frankfurt School can help to make sense of the material and enrich discussion of the issues which crop up in that course. I shall explain who the Frankfurt School were. I am not assuming any knowledge on your part where the Frankfurt School is concerned, but I will be assuming some knowledge of Marx, Nietzsche, and Freud, and some of the literary authors as well, and I will tell you later on which works of literature would be relevant to have read for the later lectures in this course. I shall then give the title, and the briefest description of the rest of the lectures in the series. You may be aware that, for various reasons which have nothing to do with me, even the title of this course was not included in the lecture list for this term. I hope some of you have seen the posters which list the lectures, but I will go through them one by one and tell you what they will be and the date I will be giving them. In the second half of the lecture, I will discuss in very general terms the influence of Marx, Nietzsche, and Freud on the Frankfurt School, to show how the School interpreted these thinkers so as to develop a radical and sociological theory of culture and mode of literary analysis.

The course Modern European Mind is traditionally divided into two parts. The first part has been called 'Diagnosis', and the second part has been called 'Expression'. In the first part, 'Diagnosis', the central authors are usually Marx, Nietzsche, and Freud. In the second part, there is usually a large choice of authors, but for our purposes, in this lecture course, we shall be most interested in the German authors – that is, Thomas Mann, Franz Kafka, and Bertolt Brecht – but also the English [language], or French writer, depending on which language you read him in, Samuel Beckett. Sometimes, the first part of the course is called 'Ideas' – the 'Mind' part of Modern European Mind; and sometimes the second part is called 'Literature' – the 'Modern' part of Modern European Mind. However, it is quite impossible to maintain these distinctions, between diagnosis and expression, or ideas and literature, in the very trivial sense that all the theorists were distinguished and original writers, and all the artists were deeply influenced by the theorists – but in much deeper senses too, of which it is the aim of this lecture course to bring out and establish.

There is one major rival in the search for the unity of Modern European Mind, and that is existentialism, for the major existentialist thinkers – Sartre and Camus – also wrote novels and plays. Existentialist readings have been developed of the philosophers in the course – of Marx, Nietzsche, and Freud – and of the novels and plays of Beckett and Kafka, often by stressing the centrality of aliena-tion. The Frankfurt School were contemporaries of Husserl, Heidegger, Sartre, and Camus. Their philosophical and literary theory was developed in opposition to phenomenology and existentialism – in opposition to what they considered to be its lack of historical, political, and social awareness. They also opposed existential read-ings of Beckett and Kafka. In the course of these lectures, I hope to discuss this opposition between these two rival schools.

Who were the Frankfurt School? They were a group of Marxist philosophers, economists, political theorists, critics, and artists who were members of the Institute for Social Research. This Institute was set up in Frankfurt, in 1923, in Germany. (I've put some of the names on the board, and I've marked those three people who we're concerned with who were never actually members of the Institute [Georg Lukács, Walter Benjamin, and Ernst Bloch], although they were closely asso-ciated, especially Ernst Bloch.) The Institute was set up with a specific aim of giving support for the Workers' Movement in Germany after the First World War. The aim was to develop interdisciplinary research within a Marxist framework. The Institute in the '20s and '30s published two very famous journals, one of which was called *The Journal for Social Research*. (It was given a very bland sort of social research title, in spite of the fact that it was a Marxist journal. I'll discuss that more in later lectures). Max Horkheimer became the director of the Institute in 1929, only four years before Hitler came to power.[2] In the early '30s the Institute went into exile, first of all in Switzerland and France, but very soon re-established in New York. Although we think of it as a very German phenomenon, it is important to realise that, really for the first twenty years of their existence, the Frankfurt School were not in Germany. In the '40s, most of the members of the School, like most of many other German émigré intellectuals, went to live in California. During the time in America, some members of the School became closer together, and some became further apart, so that, at the end of the war, at the end of the '40s, many members decided to stay in America, particularly two you have maybe heard of: Marcuse and Fromm. But Max Horkheimer and Theodor W. Adorno went back to Germany, and they set up the Institute again in Frankfurt. This time, instead of being outside the academic system, they also became professors of philosophy and sociology at the university in Frankfurt.[3]

Several of the people we shall look at were never members of the Institute, but all of them, except Bertolt Brecht (and I'll explain why he's different later on), were associated with what has come to be known as Critical Theory or Critical Marxism. What is Critical Theory or Critical Marxism? Its founder could be said to be Georg Lukács, and that's why Lukács is relevant to this lecture series. The time of its founding could be said to be just after the First World War.

2 Horkheimer became the director of the Institute in 1930. See note 12 on p. 133 of Martin Jay's afterword.

3 Adorno only became a full professor in July 1957, and then not without anti-Semitic resentment on the part of colleagues who considered his appointment favouritism by Horkheimer towards his Jewish friend. See Stefan Müller-Doohm, *Adorno: A Biography*, transl. Rodney Livingstone (Cambridge: Polity, 2005), pp. 368–9.

It's important to realise that this was a very revolutionary period. In the period between 1918 and 1920, there were revolutions in Russia, Germany, and Hungary, and it wasn't clear at that period which revolutions would succeed, and which would fail. The basic thesis of what is known as Critical Theory was developed in opposition to the Marxism of the pre-war period. This Marxism was associated with the Second International – I'm not sure if you know what the Second International was, but it was an annual meeting of representatives of socialist parties from all over Europe – and the Marxism especially of the German Social Democratic Party of the pre-war period.[4] This brand of Marxism, to use the words of Marx's first thesis on Feuerbach, had 'the chief defect of all hitherto existing materialism . . . that the thing, reality, sensuousness, or society, is conceived only in the form of the object of contemplation, but not as human sensuous activity, as practice, subjectively.'[5] By giving this quotation, what I mean to stress is that Marxists like Lukács and Karl Korsch believed that this Marxism had become passive, deterministic, positivist, and descriptive – in short, established and orthodox.[6] Instead, it was necessary, according to Lukács and Korsch, to recover Marx's intention by restoring the emphasis on praxis, and on human subjectivity, so that Marxism could become again a theory of revolution. But – and this is the crucial point really, for the future works we will be looking at – if social analysis revealed that the revolutionary subject was not emerging, or if the revolutionary subject had been defeated, then it was necessary to examine the causes of this by persistent critique of the

4   The Second International was in fact more than an annual meeting. As Martin Jay notes in his afterword to this volume, it had a permanent executive from 1900 called the International Socialist Bureau.

5   Karl Marx, 'Theses on Feuerbach', in Karl Marx and Frederick Engels, *Collected Works* (London: Lawrence & Wishart, 1975) (henceforth *MECW*), vol. 5, p. 6. Rose's translation.

6   Lukács also offered a defence of orthodox Marxism, but reclaimed the term to refer not to 'the uncritical acceptance of the results of Marx's investigations', 'not the "belief" in this or that thesis, nor the exegesis of a "sacred" book', but instead 'exclusively' to the validity of Marx's method. See Georg Lukács, 'What Is Orthodox Marxism?', in *History and Class Consciousness: Studies in Marxist Dialectics*, transl. Rodney Livingstone (London: Merlin, 2010), p. 1.

new forms of domination. Lukács, Korsch, and the Frankfurt School after them believed that the new forms of domination were not only economic and political, but also cultural. The cultural had become political (to paraphrase a sentence that I think is now used by feminism: The personal has become political).

Critical Theory is really a shorthand for this position, and it was resolutely opposed to definitions of Marxism as a science. They did not accept the idea that Marxism was like a natural science. Marxism had to resolutely subject itself to criticism in order to remain active and revolutionary, and not passive and orthodox. Two further implications of this position, which are very relevant for our concerns, is that the Frankfurt School did not only draw on Marx, but they drew also on Nietzsche and Freud as major critiques of culture of their age, to develop integral theories of social and cultural change in the first half of the twentieth century. They weren't just interested in Marx, they were interested in using the insights of other critics of capitalism.

Another implication of their position is that they applied these theories to the analysis of the works of their contemporaries – that is, to the work of Kafka, Mann, Beckett, and to the development of jazz, and other forms of mass media. As you can see, I'm stressing that, at this time, Kafka, Mann, and Beckett were contemporaries of these Marxist theorists. In a simple sense, the Frankfurt School, therefore, may be seen as the bridge over the Modern European Mind chasm, because on the one hand, its members were deeply influenced by Marx, Nietzsche, and Freud, and on the other hand, they were devoted to developing a Marxist aesthetic, and did so largely by polemics over the works of Kafka, Beckett, and Mann.

But there are further senses in which the Frankfurt School, or rather these particular individuals who we will explore in this course, are of interest to us in this connection. With the exception of Lúkacs, Horkheimer, and Marcuse, all the others were artists as well as Marxist theorists and literary critics. I don't know if you realised that. Bloch was a composer,[7] Benjamin wrote short stories, Brecht – as I'm

---

7   This is an error. As Martin Jay notes, Rose is probably confusing Ernst Bloch with the composer Ernest Bloch.

sure you know – wrote poems and plays, and Adorno was a composer.[8] They worked together on their art, as well as on their theory, and
they collaborated with other artists. For example, during the '40s, in
Los Angeles, just outside Hollywood in fact, Schoenberg, Stravinsky,
Thomas Mann, Lion Feuchtwanger, Hanns Eisler, Brecht, Horkheimer,
and Adorno were all neighbours. Lukács at that point was in Russia.
(That's really the joke actually, but I'll explain more about that later
on.) At various times, Adorno worked closely with Thomas Mann on
his novel *Doctor Faustus*.[9] Bloch worked closely with Hanns Eisler,
the composer. I don't know if you've heard of Hanns Eisler. He's a very
interesting character. He started off as a pupil of Schoenberg in
Vienna, and, later on, he became a collaborator of Brecht, so he's very
interesting for this dispute or polemic between Adorno and
Schoenberg, on the one hand, and Brecht, on the other, which we will
be going into later in this lecture series. And Benjamin, as you may
know, worked closely with Brecht.

Now, what provided the basis of these common interests and
involvements? Well, it was the belief, which they all shared, that they
faced the same dilemma as Marxists that they faced as artists. Art like
Marxism, Marxism like art, must modernise itself if it was to continue
to have any importance in face of colossal political and social change.
They differed, and they differed often bitterly, over how this modernisation should be achieved. But they all applied their principles of
innovation to both their theoretical and their artistic work.

What was that political and social change in the first thirty years of
the twentieth century which impressed them so much? I'm sure you
know, but I'll just sum up some of the major factors. On the one hand:

---

8   In a letter to Thomas Mann, introducing himself, Adorno wrote: 'I studied
philosophy and music. Instead of deciding exclusively for one subject or the other, I
have always had the feeling that my real vocation was to pursue one and the same
thing in both domains.' Theodor W. Adorno to Thomas Mann, Los Angeles, 5 July
1948, in Theodor W. Adorno and Thomas Mann, *Correspondence, 1943–1955*, ed.
Christoph Gödde and Thomas Sprecher, transl. Nicholas Walker (London: Polity,
2006), p. 24.
9   Thomas Mann, *Doctor Faustus: The Life of the German Composer Adrian
Leverkühn as Told by a Friend*, transl. James E. Woods (London: Vintage, 1999).

- The immense industrial and technological development of capitalism in Germany, and also, especially, in Russia. I don't mean
  by that so much the development of capitalism, but the emphasis
  on the immense technological developments in the first thirty
  years of the twentieth century.
- The devastation of the First World War. You may well know that
  many people in Germany, even quite radical artists and thinkers,
  were initially very excited by the First World War, and it was
  only when the war was protracted for many years that they
  became disillusioned with it, and started to support the idea of a
  democratic government in Germany.
- The failure of the German Revolution, 1918–1920: a period of
  unrest which had awakened many hopes among the communists and the socialists.
- The Stalinisation of the revolution which *did* succeed: the
  Russian Revolution.
- And, of course, the rise of fascism in Germany and Italy.

On the other hand: The cultural responses to these events. The various artistic and literary movements which developed during the First
World War, the Weimar period, and in Russia. There were several of
these movements. I want to keep them separate. We have Dada and
Surrealism; expressionism; *Neue Sachlichkeit*, which can be translated as New Objectivity; and *Proletkult* (I'm not sure how to translate
that, but you can work out what it means), in Russia. Now I've written
those up because all of these movements have come to be lumped
together under the title 'modernism'. But, originally, they were quite
separate movements, and they were all based on different theories of
the relationship between art and society, and they were originally
linked too, to debates over socialism or communism. During the
course of this lecture series, I'm going to go into each of these and
explain what they were and who was linked with them and how they
link up with the Frankfurt School. The point I would like to make
today is that what has come down to us now as debates over modernism and realism (for example, in Lukács's book *The Meaning of
Contemporary Realism*), you'll find that realism is contrasted with

modernism; but, in fact, in the original debates, when Lukács first wrote the articles that went into that book, he didn't use the word modernism; he either used 'expressionism', or 'Surrealism', or one of these other words – and we're going to see what the differences between them were.[10]

All the people we are concerned with had to make the decision when Hitler came to power in the '30s whether to go East or West, whether to go to Moscow or New York. They all debated as theorists over whether expressionism and the other modernist movements with which they had connections as artists had contributed to the rise of fascism. After the war, they had to decide again whether to go East or West, to East Germany or to West Germany. And they also had to decide how to write poetry after Auschwitz (that's a quotation from Adorno).[11] The point I'm trying to make is that all of these people had had to define their position in relation to Stalinism and to fascism, and to make up their minds after the war about the possibility or impossibility of a post-Stalinist and -fascist world.

Another offshoot, therefore, of this lecture series will be to try and break down what is known as modernism into its different original forms. This will also enable us not only to see the political and historical connections, but to discuss, for example, the relationship of Thomas Mann to expressionism, or of Franz Kafka to Surrealism. But it is also to show that the theorists themselves were involved in the expressionist movement, and other modernism movements, qua theorists, not only as artists – or rather, both as artists and as theorists. Thus, a central aim of this lecture series is to put the debates over literary modernism and Marxist theory into their historical and political context, in order to show that that context is the same for both debates. This is not in order to prove their limited historical

---

10   Georg Lukács, *The Meaning of Contemporary Realism*, transl. John and Necke Mander (London: Merlin, 1969), pp. 47–92.

11   Rose is referencing Adorno's famous aphorism: 'To write poetry after Auschwitz is barbaric.' He first made this claim in his 1949 essay, 'Cultural Criticism and Society', and then repeatedly returned to and qualified it throughout his career. Theodor W. Adorno, 'Cultural Criticism and Society', in *Prisms*, transl. Samuel and Shierry Weber (Cambridge, MA: MIT Press, 1983), p. 34.

interest, but as the best way of arguing for the continuing importance of these issues. Therefore, the lectures in this series will emphasise the political and social context of aesthetic debate. The lectures will be organised around the connections between political choice, philosophy of history, and literary analysis.

I'll now give the titles and dates and brief descriptions of the other lectures in the series:

Next week, February 1, the lecture is called 'The Politics of Realism: Georg Lukács'. In this lecture I will discuss the early pre-Marxist works of Lukács because, paradoxically enough, it was his pre-Marxist writings which had most effect on the Marxist work of the rest of the Frankfurt School. I will discuss the relationship between his major work, *History and Class Consciousness*, and the Russian and Hungarian Revolutions. I will then go on to discuss his later theory of bourgeois and socialist realism, and his relationship to Stalinism, because, you may know, from the '20s onwards, Lukács was in Russia.

February 8, the lecture is called 'The Greatness and Decline of Expressionism: Ernst Bloch'. That title actually is the title of a lecture by Lukács, but it's quite good for summing up Bloch's position. I suspect you know least about Bloch – I will tell you much more about him. Bloch was a close friend of Lukács during the First World War, but he later became a bitter enemy of Lukács's position in the 1930s. He opposed Lukács's ideas over the relationship between politics and art. I will also discuss Bloch's definition of expressionism or modernism, and his analysis of the relationship between fascism and art, which was one of his major concerns.

On February 15, the lecture will be called 'The Battle Over Walter Benjamin'. In this lecture I will discuss Benjamin's Marxist philosophy of history, his analysis of tragedy, which draws a lot on Nietzsche's book *The Birth of Tragedy* (which I expect some of you have read), and his subsequent analysis of the history of modernism.[12] I will also

---

12   Friedrich Nietzsche, *The Birth of Tragedy*, transl. Ronald Spiers, ed. Raymond Geuss and Ronald Spiers (Cambridge: Cambridge University Press, 2004).

discuss – because it links Benjamin with the rest of the Frankfurt School – the political and intellectual basis of different interpretations of Walter Benjamin. Walter Benjamin has been claimed by many different parties, and I will try and explain what the issues are in the battle over the heritage of Walter Benjamin.

The week after February 15 will be a reading week, so the next lecture will be on March 1. This lecture is entitled 'The Dialectic of Enlightenment'. That's the title of a book by Max Horkheimer and Theodor W. Adorno.[13] Perhaps some of you will look at it. This book is a very central work for the Frankfurt School. In it, Horkheimer and Adorno developed their critique of Marx, their own philosophy of history; they developed their theory of what they call 'the culture industry'; and they discussed mass society. We will discuss those issues, and I will try and correct some of the misconceptions about this particular book.

On March 8, the lecture is entitled 'Liquidating Aesthetics: Bertolt Brecht'. That is also the title of an article by Brecht, which is translated. It appears in the *Brecht on Theatre* book, edited by Willett, which I think is on the list.[14] In this lecture, we will look at Brecht's critique of Lukács's notions of bourgeois and socialist realism. We will compare Brecht's critique of traditional aesthetics with the critique of traditional aesthetics developed by the rest of the Frankfurt School. So we're not going to be considering Brecht as a whole, but particularly Brecht's polemics, discussions, and arguments with the rest of the Frankfurt School.

On March 15, the lecture is called 'The Search for Style: Theodor W. Adorno'. As you can see, I am, in a sense, giving Adorno the last word. This is partly because Adorno criticised everybody else. He criticised Lukács's concept of realism, he criticised Brecht's concept of

---

13 Theodor W. Adorno and Max Horkheimer, *Dialectic of Enlightenment: Philosophical Fragments*, transl. Edmund Jephcott, ed. Gunzelin Schmid Noerr (Stanford, CA: Stanford University Press, 2002).

14 This article took the form of an open letter to 'Mr X' (Professor Fritz Sternberg), first published in the *Berliner-Börsen Courier*, 1927. Bertolt Brecht, 'Shouldn't We Abolish Aesthetics?', in *Brecht on Theatre: The Development of an Aesthetic*, ed. and transl. John Willet (London: Eyre Methuen, 1964), pp. 20–2.

the epic theatre, and he criticised Benjamin's history of modernism. In the place of these theories, he developed his own aesthetics, which was designed to show the reproduction of contradictions in both so-called popular culture and in modernism, or expressionism.

The final lecture, if any of us are still up to it, on March 22, is entitled 'Franz Kafka or Thomas Mann'.[15] Some of you may know that this is the title of an essay by Lukács which appears in his book *The Meaning of Contemporary Realism*.[16] Franz Kafka stands, in Lukács's mind, for modernism, and Thomas Mann, for realism. In this last lecture, what I will attempt to do is to rewrite that essay, by way of illustrating and summing up the discussion of the previous weeks, and show all the different views on these issues in relationship to Lukács's original posing of the question. I will try and show how the different views we have been discussing in the previous weeks have implications for our understanding and analysis of literary texts. If you're interested in reading some Kafka or Thomas Mann, the Thomas Mann which is most relevant to read is his most difficult and challenging book, but by far the most worthwhile one, and that is *Doctor Faustus*; and with Kafka, it will be good to have read *The Trial*.[17]

For the rest of the time today, I wish to discuss the general features of the Frankfurt School's reception and interpretation of Marx, Nietzsche, and Freud, which underlie the various debates over aesthetics which we will be discussing in subsequent weeks. As I said at the beginning, I am assuming a basic acquaintance with Marx, Nietzsche, and Freud, and I will just be stressing the aspects which are most relevant for the Frankfurt School.

Basically, the Frankfurt School used Marx to develop a theory of culture which analysed the changes in the objective features of capitalism. They called this the increase in reification. And Nietzsche's

---

15 In the end, Rose combined these two lectures ('The Search for Style' and 'Franza Kafka or Thomas Mann') into one.

16 Georg Lukács, 'Franz Kafka or Thomas Mann', in *Meaning of Contemporary Realism*, pp. 47–92.

17 Franz Kafka, *The Trial*, transl. Mike Mitchell (Oxford: Oxford University Press, 2009).

and Freud's ideas were developed to criticise the traditional concept of the subject or the individual in philosophical idealism and in earlier Marxist theory. A theory of literary production and reception was developed on these bases.

Firstly, Marx. Although the concept of different forms of culture succeeding each other in history is central to Hegel, its place is taken in Marx's thought by different social forms, determined by the successive modes of production. Marx had no theory of culture as such. As I've said, Hegel did, and it was the basis of his philosophy of history.[18] In the later nineteenth century, Marx's perspective became rigidified into static, mechanistic, and deterministic distinctions between the economic base and the ideological, legal, and political superstructure. The Frankfurt School reverted to a dynamic distinction between social processes and resultant social forms by taking as their model of culture and ideology not a distinction between base and superstructure but Marx's theory of commodity fetishism, and this theory received its classic statement in *Capital* volume 1, chapter 1, and throughout the *Grundrisse*. (You've probably heard of sexual fetishism, but not commodity fetishism.) There's a section in *Capital*, chapter 1, volume 1, actually called 'Commodity Fetishism' ['The Fetishism of the Commodity and Its Secret'], but there's a lot on commodity fetishism in the *Grundrisse*, and sometimes people find that, well, Marx expatiates more in the *Grundrisse* than in *Capital*.

---

18   This would become one of the major arguments of Rose's *Hegel Contra Sociology* (1981), and the crux of her critique of Marx. For instance: 'Missing from Marx's *oeuvre* is any concept of culture, of formation and re-formation (*Bildung*). There is no idea of a vocation which may be assimilated or re-formed by the determinations or law which it fails to acknowledge or the strength of which it underestimates. Because Marx did not relate actuality to representation and subjectivity, his account of structural change in capitalism is abstractly related to possible change in consciousness. This resulted in gross oversimplification regarding the likelihood and the inhibition of change. This is not the argument that Marx's predictions about the conditions of the formation of revolutionary consciousness were wrong. It is an argument to the effect that the very concept of consciousness and, *a fortiori*, of revolutionary consciousness, are insufficiently established in Marx.' Gillian Rose, 'The Culture and Fate of Marxism', in *Hegel Contra Sociology* (London: Verso, 2009), pp. 233–4.

I'm now going to try and outline very roughly indeed what Marx's theory of commodity fetishism is. If you don't know it, then I would recommend you look at these few pages in *Capital*, volume 1.[19]

Commodities, according to Marx, are produced in a society in which labour power is sold for a wage, and surplus value is realised when the product of that labour is sold, not by the worker, but by the entrepreneur or the employer for a profit. This is by contrast with a pre-capitalist society or a non-capitalist society in which the direct producer or worker would either consume or sell the product of his labour himself. He would not be selling his labour power, and he would be realising directly the value incorporated in the product. Thus, a commodity, that is, a product produced under capitalist conditions, consists of two components: its use value, and its exchange value. Its use value, which Marx also calls its value in use, means its specific qualities. For example, the taste of an apple, or the warmth of the coat which you wear. The exchange value, by contrast, is what a commodity is equivalent to as a ratio of another commodity, usually expressed in money. So, one is a ratio, and the other is the concrete qualities of a product. A result of this divorce between use and exchange is that exchange value seems to be a characteristic of the product itself – that is, its price. People think that value inheres in the product itself, and they do not understand that in fact it is the expression of specific social relations and activities between people. Marx says, 'The social character of activity, as well as the social form of the product, and the share of individuals in production, here appear in the commodity as something alien and objective.'[20] 'A definite social relation between men assumes the phantasmagoric form of a relation between things.'[21] That's the crucial sentence. This is what Marx calls fetishism – that is, when you treat something as a thing in itself, when in fact it is the expression of determinate social relations between people.

---

19   Karl Marx, *Capital: A Critique of Political Economy*, vol. 1, transl. Ben Fowkes (London: Penguin, 1976), pp. 163–77.

20   Karl Marx, *Grundrisse: Foundations of the Critique of Political Economy (Rough Draft)*, transl. Martin Nicolaus (London: Penguin, 1993), p. 157.

21   'It is nothing but the definite social relation between men themselves which assumes here, for them, the fantastic form of a relation between things.' Marx, *Capital*, vol. 1, p. 165.

The Frankfurt School believed that this idea that real social relations between people are transformed into and misunderstood as relations between things provided a model for the relationship between social processes and social institutions and consciousness. This model, unlike the distinction between economic base and ideological superstructure, would not reduce institutional and ideological formations to mere epiphenomena or to simple reflections of a base. It would provide a sociological explanation for the social determination yet relative autonomy of other social forms, such as culture. It provided a way of saying that something is both socially determined and yet also partially autonomous. Marx is not saying, for example, that the illusions that arise out of commodity fetishism are wrong; he is saying that those illusions are necessary and real, but nevertheless, they are illusions. This is what the Frankfurt School from Lukács onwards called 'reification' – a term which Marx himself did not use, although for various reasons it has become associated with Marx himself. In fact, their adoption of this notion of reification gave the different members of the Frankfurt School enormous liberty to interpret Marx differently. Even the theory of commodity fetishism came to support quite different philosophies of history, and quite different political positions and theories of culture. That's all I'm going to say about their general adaptation of Marx, for the moment.

I'll now say something about the Frankfurt School's interest in Nietzsche. It is a commonplace that Nietzsche's ideas have been abused by twentieth-century social theorists and politicians of the right. For example, you may have heard of Oswald Spengler or Ernst Jünger. But it is not so generally known that Nietzsche had an enormous influence on twentieth-century theorists of the left. Among those we are particularly concerned with, it is especially true of Bloch, Horkheimer, Benjamin, and Adorno. Why were they interested in Nietzsche? They were interested in Nietzsche for a number of reasons, and I will list them quite briefly:

- Nietzsche rejected a philosophy of history based on the Hegelian idea of an ultimate *telos* or goal in history, of an ideal society in the future, or of the reconciliation of all contradictions. Nietzsche rejected that position. He applied the notion of contradiction to the optimistic philosophy of history itself – for example, that the process of historical change might turn into the opposite of all the ideals. This is what Horkheimer and Adorno were later to call 'the dialectic of Enlightenment'.

- They were interested in Nietzsche because Nietzsche criticised the traditional philosophical concept of the subject. This traditional philosophical concept of the subject which had also been adopted by certain forms of Marxism, for example the existentialist interpretation of Marxism, is that the unity of consciousness is the basis of all reality. The Frankfurt School, on the contrary, believed that social reality could not be reduced to the sum of facts of consciousness. They used this point to emphasise both that social reality cannot be reduced to people's consciousness of it, but that the analysis of social determination of forms of subjectivity is essential: that subjectivity is a social category.

- A third reason why they were interested in Nietzsche is that Nietzsche's thought is based on the idea of will to power. The Frankfurt School, too, were interested in analysing new forms of anonymous and universal political and cultural domination which affect everyone equally, and which prevent the formation of classic liberating proletarian class consciousness.

- Fourthly, they were interested in Nietzsche because Nietzsche launched an attack on the bourgeois culture of his day. Like Marx, he referred to 'bourgeois philistinism'. The Frankfurt School, too, wanted to demonstrate the re-emergence of social contradictions in both so-called popular and so-called serious culture. They were equally critical of both high-brow and low-brow, if you like. In fact, they rejected that distinction.

- The final reason the Frankfurt School were interested in Nietzsche is that Nietzsche produced an analysis of the birth of tragedy in Greek society, which was radically sociological, and which, unlike the earlier tradition in German thought, did not idealise Greek society. This provided a model for the Frankfurt School's analyses of literary genres in advanced capitalist society. The Frankfurt School put their emphasis on literary form, not content.

Finally, I'd just like to say a few words about the Frankfurt School's interest in Freud. If a traditional concept of the subject was unacceptable, what was to take its place? The Frankfurt School used Freudian theory to explicate the social formation of subjectivity and its contradictions in advanced capitalist society. They thought that psychoanalytic theory would provide the connection between economic and political processes and resultant cultural forms. But they did not turn to Freud's later, more obviously and directly sociological works, which you may have read in Modern European Mind, such as *Civilisation and Its Discontents*.[22] They based their interpretation on an analysis of Freud's most central psychoanalytic concepts. They were particularly attracted to Freud's position that individuality was a formation, an achievement, not an absolute, or a given. They wished to develop a theory of the loss of autonomy or decline of the individual in advanced capitalist society which would not idealise what had counted as autonomy or individuality in the first place. They used Freudian theory in many of their major studies: in their studies of the acceptance and reproduction of authority in late capitalist society; in their examination and attempts to account for the success of fascism; in their development of a concept of the culture industry, and its influence on people's consciousness and unconsciousness; and finally, in the general enquiry into the possibility or impossibility of cultural and aesthetic experience in late capitalist society.

That's really all for today. In subsequent lectures I shall be stressing the differences between the various thinkers. If anybody would like to ask any questions now, I'd be very happy to answer them.

---

22   Sigmund Freud, *Civilization and Its Discontents*, transl. David McLintock (London: Penguin, 2002).

2

The Politics of Realism: Georg Lukács

[In this lecture I will look at the early and the late work of the Hungarian philosopher and literary critic, Georg Lukács. I will show] how his early work had a stimulating and liberating effect on Marxism, and specifically on the Frankfurt School, on the people we will be discussing in the rest of these lectures; and how his later work had a deadening and restricting effect, and how the rest of the Frankfurt School rejected it.[1] These changes in Lukács's position can be related to the political decisions which he made – to his relationship to the Russian Revolution, and to his analysis of fascism. Both of these positions were rejected by the rest of the Frankfurt School. In the course of discussing the development of Lukács's views on modernism, I am going to make good on my promise from last week, and break down modernism into its original constituent components. Last week I said that Lukács referred to 'modernism', but under 'modernism' he lumped together a lot of different movements. This week I am going to try and tell you a little bit about expressionism and *Proletkult*, because those who disagreed with Lukács refused to lump together all these movements under the title 'modernism'. The other ones I

---

1 The recording starts a few seconds after the lecture begins. The contents of the squared brackets are interpolated by the editors.

mentioned, which we will also be talking about in subsequent weeks, were Surrealism and Dada, and this other movement called *Neue Sachlichkeit*, or New Objectivity – but they're not so important for this week. As you can see from these introductory remarks, I am not going to give Lukács an easy time of it. I am not going to try and be fair to Lukács. I am going to examine Lukács with a view to what has been seen as his importance for subsequent Marxist literary criticism.

I've put on the board an outline of Lukács's life. The aim of this is to show you how many different places he lived, and how many different debates and political movements he was involved in. They're just the main dates, but I will go through them now.

Lukács was born in Hungary in 1885. He first studied in Hungary, but he went on to complete his studies in Germany. At Berlin University and Heidelberg University he met Georg Simmel, Ernst Bloch, Max Weber, and Emil Lask.[2] These people were sociologists and philosophers. Some of them you probably know of. Simmel is a famous sociologist, and so is Weber. It was in Germany that his friendship with Ernst Bloch, who I'll be talking about next week, developed. The other people I mentioned were neo-Kantian philosophers, but they are not important for our purposes. In 1918, Lukács went back to Hungary and joined the Communist Party. He took part in the revolution in Hungary in 1918 and 1919, and he became the minister for cultural affairs. He tried to put his revolutionary culturism into practice. I'll tell you a bit more about that later on. He was very involved in this revolution, but the revolution was defeated in the same year.[3]

---

2   Georg Simmel (1858–1918) was a German sociologist and essayist. Ernst Bloch (1885–1987) was a Marxist Hegelian philosopher. Max Weber (1864–1920) was a German sociologist and historian. And Emil Lask (1875–1915) was a neo-Kantian philosopher of the Southwestern school.

3   The Hungarian Soviet Republic lasted from 21 March to 1 August 1919, when it was crushed by counterrevolutionary forces with backing from the Romanian army. Most of the communist leadership immediately escaped to Vienna, but Lukács stayed in an attempt to reorganise the movement. After this failed, he followed to Vienna.

Lukács fled to Vienna. It was during his time in Vienna, in the '20s, that he wrote his famous *History and Class Consciousness*. And, in fact, although he stayed in Vienna until 1929, during the '20s he increasingly accepted the Comintern, the Russian line. He accepted the criticism of his books from Russia, and you may know that, in 1924, he recanted some of the views in that book which had been attacked by people associated closely with the Russian government.[4] This culminated in his going to Moscow in 1929. This is very important, as you'll see, for his increasingly dominant role in discussions over both *Proletkult* and expressionism (*Proletkult* was started in Russia). But he went back to Berlin, from 1931 to 1933, and he was a founding member of the League of Proletarian Revolutionary Writers. This was a group of writers who were members of the Communist Party, and who developed a league which was very short lived actually, because most of them fled to Moscow in 1933. They had a journal called *Die Linkskurve*, or 'The left curve', and I'm going to be telling you more about this in a minute, when I go on to discuss *Proletkult*. Although we think of Lukács as having been in Moscow in the '20s and '30s, it is important to know that he returned to Berlin for those few years and dominated the discussion in Germany as well. Then he went back to Moscow in 1933, and ten years later, at the end of the '30s, he became involved in the Popular Front, in its literary wing, and he edited the journal *Das Wort* (The word).[5] The Popular Front was a union of communist and socialist democratic writers and politicians in the fight against fascism, and, as I say, Lukács was dominant in the literary wing of this. Brecht was another editor of this journal, *Das Wort*.

After the war, [Lukács] returned to Hungary, and became a professor at the University of Budapest. From 1945 onwards, there were several

---

4   *History and Class Consciousness* was denounced in 1924 by the Executive Committee of the Fifth Comintern Congress in Moscow as unorthodox and revisionist Marxism. In fact, Lukács did not formally recant until 1933, in the autobiographical text 'My Road to Marx'. Georg Lukács, 'Mein Weg zu Marx', *Internationale Literatur* 2 (1933), pp. 185–7 – reprinted in *Schriften zur Ideologie und Politik* (Neuwied: Luchterhand, 1967), pp. 323–9.

5   This is an error: while Lukács was involved with *Das Wort*, he was never one of its editors.

periods when Lukács was attacked by the Communist Party. His relationship to Stalinism is ambiguous. I'm going to go into that in a minute
as well. But he wasn't always in favour. Several times, he was out of
favour, and always for his views on the relationship between literature
and society. In 1952, he wrote a book called *The Destruction of Reason*,
which is being translated into English at the moment.[6] In this book he
associated almost all previous German thought with the rise of fascism.
In 1956, he wrote the book *The Meaning of Contemporary Realism*,
which is merely a summary of views which he had been discussing and
talking about since the time of the Popular Front (1938), but also since
his time in Berlin (1931–1933).[7] By the middle of the '50s, it had become
quite acceptable to contrast realism with modernism, whereas earlier
on, Lukács had always referred to either expressionism or *Proletkult*. In
1956, Lukács was again involved in a revolution in Hungary, and when
it was crushed he had to flee for a few months. But after that he was soon
reinstated at the University, and from 1956 onwards, he became increasingly critical of Russia and of Stalinism.[8]

Now, what I want to do, because it's going to crop up throughout
the course of these lectures, is say something to you about what
expressionism is, and what *Proletkult* is. First of all, I will say a few
things about expressionism.

Expressionism was a movement which involved painters, poets,
playwrights, and essayists. It's usually dated most strictly from about
1905 to 1920/21. Where painters are concerned, it is associated with
two groups of painters, one of which was founded in Dresden in

---

6   This translation of *Die Zerstörung der Vernunft* was published in 1980. Georg
Lúkacs, *The Destruction of Reason*, transl. Peter Palmer (London: Merlin, 1980).

7   *The Meaning of Contemporary Realism* was first published in 1958. The first
English translation, by John and Necke Mander, was published in 1963 by the Merlin
Press.

8   Lukács played an important role in the anti-Stalinist sentiment that preceded
the October 1956 Hungarian Revolution, which sought to combat the Soviet control
of Hungary. When the revolution was briefly successful, Lukács was on the governing
Central Committee as minister of culture. However, in November 1956 the Soviet
Union invaded Budapest and Lukács, along with the rest of Nagy's government, was
deported to Romania. Lukács was one of a few not to be executed.

1905, called *Die Brücke*, 'The bridge'. The best-known members of this group were Ernst Kirchner and Emil Nolde.[9] Another group of painters were put together in 1909 in Munich, and they called themselves *Der Blaue Reiter*, 'The blue rider'. The most famous of those were Kandinsky, Paul Klee, and Franz Marc.[10] In the realm of poetry, expressionism is associated with a very famous anthology of poems which was published in 1919 called *Menschheitsdämmerung*, which means 'Twilight of mankind'. This was a reference to Nietzsche's work *Götzen-Dämmerung*, or 'Twilight of the idols'. This anthology was a collection of poems which had been published between 1910 and 1920, and the best-known people in it were Franz Werfel and Gottfried Benn.[11] Expressionism was also associated with periodicals and journals, with cultural criticism and essayism. As I said last week, many of the members of the Frankfurt School considered themselves originally to be expressionists.[12]

What did these people stand for? What did they consider united them? On the negative side, they were opposed to conventional notions of representation in art. They made a distinction, or rather they took up an old distinction, between *mimesis* and *Ausdruck*. *Mimesis* is a Greek word for 'imitation', and *Ausdruck* is a German word for 'expression'. They contrasted art as *mimesis* – that is, art as the imitation of nature or the social world – with *Ausdruck*, which I'll come to in a minute. Let me just say a little more about *mimesis*. They identified *mimesis* with a notion of art as imitating the natural or social world, and with a presentation of characters in literature in which the motivations of the characters are developed and the audience is encouraged to identify with them. They were also opposed to the recent development of naturalism in art, which was associated for them with scientific progress and social reform. In opposition to this, they considered themselves to be in revolt against bourgeois society,

---

9   Ernst Ludwig Kirchner (1880–1938); Emil Nolde (1867–1956).

10   Wassily Kandinsky (1866–1944); Paul Klee (1879–1940); Franz Marc (1880–1916).

11   Franz Werfel (1890–1945); Gottfried Benn (1886–1956).

12   This is particularly true of Ernst Bloch, as Rose goes on to explore in her lecture on him, 'The Greatness and Decline of Expressionism'.

against materialism, and, later on especially, against the horrors of the First World War – which, as I mentioned last week, many people had originally welcomed. There are two different interpretations of expressionism, and they sometimes presented themselves in two quite different ways. On the one hand, there was an emphasis – and this is the expression side of that dichotomy – on formlessness: the idea that art, instead of depicting social reality, would be the expression of emotion; that it would present things which were not previously art's concern: ugliness, pain, the grotesque. As a result of this, expressionist works were often considered apocalyptic and intensely subjective. There was another strain in expressionism which, far from stressing formlessness, had an even greater stress on form, on new forms in art, as a way of bringing out the traditional role of form in art, as a way of exposing the relationship between art and society. They were the different strains of expressionism, and we shall pick them up as we go along.

Another way in which expressionism was very varied was in the political contrast between different members. Some people associated with expressionism were messianic and nationalistic, and later on became involved in fascism. Other expressionists were socialists – they were activist and revolutionary. An example of that wing is Heinrich Mann, or Ernst Toller.[13] An example of the nationalist or messianic wing is Gottfried Benn. Now, in fact, when the Nazi Party came to power, they were quite opposed to expressionism. The fascists were opposed to expressionism, and in 1937 the Nazis mounted an exhibition of what they called 'degenerate art', in Munich, in which they exhibited expressionist works. But, in spite of the fact that the Nazis and fascists were generally opposed to expressionism, Lukács linked fascism and expressionism on the basis of a charge of its social irresponsibility. It wasn't only Lukács who did this. Many other ex-expressionist poets, members of the Communist Party, did so too. These were the people who, in 1933, went to Moscow. You may remember last week we mentioned that people made very different decisions, whether they went East or West in 1933.

---

13   Heinrich Mann (1871–1950); Ernst Toller (1893–1939).

That's a sort of potted introduction to expressionism, as one of the things which Lukács was very opposed to.

The other thing, the other debate which Lukács was involved in, and also very opposed to, was called *Proletkult*. Now, what was *Proletkult*? This was a debate which originated in Russia, but was also taken up in Germany in the '20s, over the possibility and desirability of revolutionary proletarian literature – that is, literature written for and by the working class. Now, obviously, this debate had very different parameters from those that it had in Germany. In Russia, it was the question of the possibility and desirability of proletarian art in the period of the dictatorship of the proletariat. In Germany, it was the period of advanced capitalism. In both countries, the argument usually turned on the evaluation of classical cultural heritage. In Russia, Lenin and Trotsky had both been admirers of the European classical culture, in contrast to what they saw as Russia's cultural backwardness. They were both opposed to the idea of specifically proletarian art. They considered the idea dogmatic and abstract. They believed that the old bourgeois art had expressed social truth in spite of its class character. The *Proletkult* groups, who had been in existence since about the 1890s, and who survived, incidentally, up to the rise of Stalin, were opposed to this view. They were in favour of a specifically proletarian art, to be created by experiments with form, because the old forms, the old bourgeois forms, were implicated in the old society. As a result, their expressions tended to be especially in film, but also in poetry. It often resulted in extremely formal and abstract works. In Germany, in the late '20s, this debate was taken over by the League of Proletarian Revolutionary Writers. They had an influential journal called *The Left Curve*. They continued the same debate, but of course under different conditions – under the conditions of the possibility of proletarian art under advanced capitalist society, not under the dictatorship of the proletariat, which was believed to be the situation in Russia. Although, initially, they put a stress on the desirability of proletarian art, they became opposed to other forms of innovation in Germany – that is, they were opposed to expressionist art in Germany. They considered it to be petit bourgeois, even when the artists were socialists, or even communists. The critique of innovation in Germany

– that is, the critique of expressionism in Germany – became, quite soon, a rejection of *Proletkult* innovation as well. This, I suppose, is the origin of those who were opposed to these things lumping them together, as Lukács later did. They developed – and this also occurred in Russia – the concept of socialist realism. This was based on the idea that the traditional nineteenth-century novel was more realistic, was truer to the representation of social reality, than the modern forms of montage, documentary, and alienation. We will be discussing those increasingly. Many of the contributors to this debate went to Moscow in the 1930s, and in Moscow they indicted expressionism for its contribution to fascism. Lukács, as it were, followed Lenin and Trotsky and the later Russian establishment in developing a notion of bourgeois and socialist realism, in opposition to both expressionism and *Proletkult*.

I claimed in the introduction to this lecture that there was a difference between early and late Lukács. I just want to point out what that argument is in terms of his life's movements. Up to 1926, as I said, Lukács was associated with revolutionary movements. He was frequently an exile from Hungary; he was involved in the 1918 Hungarian Revolution, and he spent the '20s in exile in Vienna. But, as I've said, from 1926 onwards he was associated with Stalinism, and the Stalinist policy of socialism in one country. He accepted the disastrous Stalinist position of the '30s – that was, Stalin prevented an effective fight against fascism by the European communist parties because he equated the fight against social-democratic parties with the fight against fascism. He called the social-democratic parties 'social fascists'. Instead of encouraging communist parties to unite with social-democratic parties to fight fascism, he prevented their doing so. Lukács didn't disown this position until the mid-'50s. Later, however, in 1938, when the Popular Front was set up from Moscow – that is, in the late '30s, when a policy of unity between social democrats and communists was developed – and published in the journal *Das Wort*, Lukács vociferously argued that expressionism and fascism were linked. He never, however, examined the implications of the Stalinist position on politics and aesthetics for the success of fascism. In fact, Brecht, who was co-editor of *Das Wort*, and who deeply disagreed with Lukács's views (we have his views now in English as well), did not publish his work at the time, because he did not want to destroy the unity of the Popular Front. But, as you can imagine, there were other people who were associated with expressionism and *Proletkult* who didn't support Stalin's position, and also, therefore, did not agree with Lukács's equating of expressionism and fascism. However, as I mentioned before, there were several periods in his life when Lukács was in disgrace in the Stalinist camp: in 1929–30, 1941, 1949–50, and after 1956, his position was unsure. What I'm trying to get at, generally, is that, from the late '20s onwards, Lukács tried to reconcile Stalinism with bourgeois democratic culture; but bourgeois democratic culture was increasingly narrowly defined by him, up to the point in *The Destruction of Reason* (1952) when he analysed Nietzsche and Freud as proto-fascists.

What I'm going to do in the second half of this lecture is compare *The Theory of the Novel* and *History and Class Consciousness* as representative of Lukács's early work, which was so important for the subsequent development of Marxist aesthetics in the Frankfurt School, with his later work.[14] 'The Old Culture and the New Culture,' which I'm taking as a later work, was in fact written at the same time as *History and Class Consciousness*.[15] But for our purposes, we can count it as a later work. First of all, what I'm going to do is state some of the central ideas in these four works, and then, by way of a conclusion, I'll sum up which aspects of these works were important for the development of Marxist aesthetics and for the Frankfurt School's ideas, and which aspects of them they rejected.[16]

The Theory of the Novel was published in parts between 1916 and 1920. This book is divided into two parts. In the first part, Lukács is concerned with the relationship between historical epochs and literary form – the relationship, for example, between Greek society, epic

---

14   Georg Lukács, *The Theory of the Novel: A Historico-philosophical Essay on the Forms of Great Epic Literature*, transl. Anna Bostock (Cambridge, MA: MIT Press, 1974).

15   Georg Lukács, 'The Old Culture and the New Culture', *Telos* 5 (1970), pp. 21–30.

16   The fourth work, unnamed here, is *Meaning of Contemporary Realism*.

poetry, and tragedy in drama. He looks at the relationship between historical epochs and literary form as a basis for the theory of the changes in social structure which have led to the rise of the novel. He draws a distinction between 'integrated' and 'disintegrated' cultures – integrated cultures being Greek and earlier societies, and disintegrated cultures being associated with the rise of the capitalist mode of production – and the resultant literary genres. This is a way of analysing modern society and innovation and literature. According to Lukács, the rise of the novel as a new cultural form is closely connected with the increase in social disunity and disharmony. He couches this thesis, though, still in predominantly metaphysical terms, because he had not yet developed his relationship with Marxism. Nevertheless, this notion of culture and disunity or disharmony was very important to the Frankfurt School's concept of culture, and very opposed to the traditional notion of culture as something unified, total, autonomous, and perfect.

The second part of this book, *The Theory of the Novel*, contains what Lukács calls a typology of the novel form – that is, an investigation of different kinds of the novel. He analyses especially the historical and social reasons for the development of what he calls modern subjectivity. We mentioned that a bit last week: the interest of Lukács and the Frankfurt School in a new concept of the subject. He looked at the relationship between what he called modern subjectivity and new kinds of artistic style. He stressed the connection between the use of irony and the novel form, and he interpreted irony as a form of critical insight into the changing relationship between social objectivity and subjectivity. He considered ironic writing to be essentially critical and activist. This is significant because Romantic irony was one of the forerunners of the modernism that Lukács despised so much. In this book, when he examined Romantic irony, he was excited by it, and saw it as progressive in literature; but, later on, modernism, which, in many ways, has things in common with Romantic irony, was one of the things which he was so critical of. We will come back to *The Theory of the Novel*, because it was a very important book for the other members of the Frankfurt School.

Now I'm going to say something about *History and Class Consciousness*, and I apologise to those of you who know the book well. *History and Class Consciousness* was a collection of essays – it wasn't written as a book – written between 1918 and 1923. I'm going to do today what people always do, and that is just discuss the first half of the book. It is the first half of the book which has given Lukács the reputation for being a Hegelian or idealist Marxist; but, in fact, if you read through the second half of the book, where he discusses questions of political organisation, the party, Rosa Luxemburg, and Lenin, you'll see that this reputation is not deserved, and that Lukács was very concerned with concrete political questions as well. The book is as Leninist as it is Hegelian.

What I'm going to do now is just very briefly mention the four important ideas in *History and Class Consciousness* on which you could say the whole tradition of the Frankfurt School is based. I'm going to go over what I said last week on commodity fetishism because several people told me that they didn't quite grasp it. The first, and to many people outrageous, thing that Lukács said in *History and Class Consciousness* was that Marxism is to be thought of as a method, and not as a set of doctrines or truths. What he said is the following: 'Even if research has disproved once and for all every one of Marx's individual theses, Marx's method remains valid.'[17] Now, there are many other people who would think that that's a destruction of Marxism. He justified this by saying that 'the dialectic' – that is, the Marxist theory – 'is not a finished theory to be applied mechanically to all the phenomena of life but only exists as theory in and through its application.'[18] Now, this definition of Marxism made Marxism appear extremely flexible, and it attracted a lot of people.

If Marxism is a method, what is this method? Lukács explicated it by using the notion of totality – that is, that the only way we can understand society is by relating individual facts to their function in

---

17   Georg Lukács, *History and Class Consciousness: Studies in Marxist Dialectics*, transl. Rodney Livingstone (London: Merlin, 2010), p. 1.
18   Georg Lukács, *Lenin: A Study on the Unity of His Thought*, transl. Nicholas Jacobs (London: Verso, 2009), p. 84.

the totality to which they belong. It's necessary to see isolated facts as part of a unified and dynamic process. But, in fact, apart from this basic emphasis on a dynamic and processual concept of society, Lukács had two concepts of totality, although of course they're linked. The first is the given totality, and the second is totality as an aim. By the given totality, Lukács meant the principle which systematically structures all social relations and forms them into a totality. The emphasis on totality means discerning what that principle is. The second notion of totality – totality as an aim – means the idea of totality as the sum of past, present, and future possibilities. Of course, if you understand totality in the first sense – that is, the principle which systematically structures social relationships – you will dissolve the apparent fixity of those relationships; you can see their social formation, and possibly the way in which they are changing. This becomes the second notion of totality: totality as an aim, or totality as the unity of the historical process.

The famous central essay in *History and Class Consciousness* is called 'Reification and the Consciousness of the Proletariat'.[19] In this essay – and this is what we touched on last week, and I will now go through that again, with special reference to Lukács. Lukács generalises Marx's theory of commodity fetishism to produce a theory of culture, unlike previous Marxist theory, which had drawn a distinction between base and superstructure in order to develop a theory of ideology.

What did Lukács understand by Marx's theory of commodity fetishism? I will repeat my explication of commodity fetishism which I gave last week: In a pre-capitalist society, the direct producer or worker would either consume or sell the product which he has produced himself. He would not be selling his labour power, and he would be realising or enjoying directly the value which he has incorporated in the product. But, in a commodity-producing society, the direct producer sells his labour power for a wage, and its value – the value of his labour – is realised or enjoyed when the product is sold

---

19   Georg Lukács, 'Reification and the Consciousness of the Proletariat', in *History and Class Consciousness*, pp. 83–222.

by the employer or entrepreneur for a profit. Thus, a commodity consists of two components: its use value, or its value in use: its specific qualities (the taste of the apple, or the warmth of the coat); and its exchange value: what a commodity is equivalent to as a ratio of other commodities, usually expressed in money. A result of this divorce between use and exchange is that exchange value seems to be a characteristic of the product itself – that is, its price – and people don't understand it as an expression of specific social relations and activity between people. Marx said: 'The social character of activity, as well as the social form of the product, and the share of individuals in production here appear as something alien and objective';[20] 'A definite social relation between men assumes the phantasmagoric form of a relation between things.'[21] This is what Marx called commodity fetishism. It is what Lukács called reification. Marx didn't call it reification, although, partly as a result of Lukács's work, we tend to think that Marx did use the word 'reification', but he didn't. As I said last week, by calling this aspect of Marx's thought 'reification', people were able to take enormous liberties with it.

Lukács went on to stress the subjective correlates of reification – that is, how people experience it, how it prevents people from understanding society, and the social forces which are structuring their lives. He particularly stressed how reification fragments social life. But there is a problem. If reification is so widespread – that is, if people misunderstand social life – how is it possible for working-class consciousness to develop? The working class, according to Lukács, is the class with the possibility of transcending reification – of seeing beyond it, in its consciousness and in its activity. Lukács called the working class 'the subject of history', by which he meant it is the class whose particular interests are really the universal interests of the whole society – that is, the universal class – unlike the bourgeoisie, which merely presents its particular interests as if they were the

---

20 Karl Marx, *Grundrisse: Foundations of the Critique of Political Economy (Rough Draft)*, transl. Martin Nicolaus (London: Penguin, 1993), p. 157.

21 Karl Marx, *Capital: A Critique of Political Economy*, vol. 1, transl. Ben Fowkes (London: Penguin, 1976), p. 165. Rose's translation.

interests of the whole society: [the perfect class consciousness] which would exist when the working class really understood its interests and acted accordingly. He called this perfect class consciousness, 'imputed class consciousness'.[22] He contrasted this ideal of imputed class consciousness with actually existing class consciousness, which could be described at any point in time, which is determined, and which is the class consciousness in which the working class does not understand its interests or act accordingly. Lukács said: 'The structure of commodity-relations yield[s] a model of all the objective forms of bourgeois society together with all the subjective forms corresponding to them.'[23] He went on to analyse reification in other areas of social life – in bureaucracy, in the legal structure of society, in the state, and in culture – as [a source of] new forms of domination in late capitalist society, which were preventing the emergence of ideal class consciousness. Thus, by generalising Marx's theory of commodity fetishism, Lukács was able to show that the dominant forces are not only economic and political, but, as I mentioned last week, that the cultural is also political. Another word that is used to describe this is 'cultural politics'.

But how did Lukács define culture? Now, we're coming on to the two later works, and you'll see, in my concluding remarks, that there's quite a big difference between what Lukács did in *History and Class Consciousness* and what he did in these two works that we're going on now to discuss. In this article, 'The Old Culture and the New Culture', Lukács defined culture as 'products and abilities separate from the immediate maintenance of life' – which was a very conventional definition.[24] Culture,

---

22   Lukács theorises 'imputed' class consciousness in the essay 'Class Consciousness', in *History and Class Consciousness*, pp. 46–82.

23   Lukács, 'Reification and the Consciousness of the Proletariat', p. 83. The full quotation reads: 'Only in this case [i.e. when the commodity is not considered in isolation] can the structure of commodity-relations be made to yield a model of all the objective forms of bourgeois society together with all the subjective forms corresponding to them.'

24   Lukács, 'The Old Culture and the New', p. 21. Lukács was delivering this essay as a lecture in 1919 when it was interrupted as the Hungarian Soviet Revolution was announced.

according to Lukács, is only possible in a society in which production is a unified and self-contained process. The capitalist mode of production, according to Lukács, destroys the previous autonomy of culture by turning cultural products into commodities, and by splitting up the work process. In the twentieth century, which he called the era of finance capital, Lukács thought culture had completely collapsed, because even the bourgeois ideology of freedom no longer exists. He believed culture would only be possible again when the rule of the economy was abolished. Lukács's concept of culture now, therefore, depends upon conditions of organic unity and a lost ideal of harmony. This view was opposed by the rest of the Frankfurt School, and I'm just going to mention this now, because we are going to be discussing it in detail in subsequent weeks. For them, the so-called autonomy of culture was only created or achieved under capitalism. Their concept of culture presupposes disunity, not unity. Lukács, from the 1930s onwards, but culminating in this book here [*The Meaning of Contemporary Realism*], which is available in English, saw all forms of modernism – that is, all forms we've put on the board, which he jolly well knew were quite different from each other, in certain respects – he saw them all as indicators of the collapse of culture.

I'm just going to mention very briefly what he developed in the place of modernism – that is, his notions of bourgeois and socialist realism. He was particularly interested in the novel, and he defended realism against what he called modernism in the novel. As an example of realism, he considered Balzac to be a classic nineteenth-century realist; and he considered – although it's quite incredible, and was challenged, not only by the rest of the Frankfurt School but by Thomas Mann himself – he considered Thomas Mann to be a realist. Where modernism is concerned, as I say, he not only meant expressionism and *Proletkult*, but by 1956 he was also lumping together Proust, Kafka, Joyce – you name it. Realism, according to Lukács, is committed to a view of man as an essentially social and political being, formed by his society and striving to attain understanding of its contradictions in order to act on it. Texts written in this tradition portray the lives of individuals firmly rooted in specified and identifiable time and space, and the complex tissue of their interaction with their environment, in a way which Lukács called 'universal' and 'concrete'. By 'universal', Lukács meant typical and also harmonious, in the sense of transcending any particular view. By 'concrete', he meant according to the real possibilities of people in the given situation. Realism, whether bourgeois or socialist, in this way, aims at what he called a 'truthful reflection' of reality. Modernism, by contrast, is based on a view which is 'by nature solitary, asocial, unable to enter into relationships with other human beings', not concerned with understanding social reality, or with acting on it.[25] Texts of this kind portray individuals ' "thrown into the world": meaninglessly, unfathomably', without any development of personality, and hence statically, and ahistorically.[26] They concentrate on the abstract potentialities of the individual's life, his rich imaginings, which are preferred to social realities. It is thus intensely subjective literature which colludes in the distortion of social reality instead of fighting it, by its obsession with styles to convey subjective experience. Lukács called such writing 'decadent', and judged that it heralded the end of literature.

In subsequent weeks, we'll go into more details of that position, and into people's criticism of it. I'd like to just use the last five minutes to contrast the difference between Lukács's earlier and later works, bringing out the importance of the earlier work, as opposed to the later work, for the Frankfurt School and for the development of a Marxist aesthetic. I've got four points here. I will give first of all the positive influence on the Frankfurt School, and in the second place, the subsequent change in Lukács's opinion on this issue, which was rejected by the Frankfurt School.

Lukács's discussion of reification extended the discussion of ideology. It developed a view which pointed to the relative autonomy of cultural forms. By stressing that reification is an obscuring force in society, it linked socially determined illusions with illusions of artistic form. It thus assumed that knowledge of society was just as problematic as knowledge of art. But, later on, Lukács dropped

---

25   Georg Lukács, 'The Ideology of Modernism', in *The Meaning of Contemporary Realism*, transl. John and Necke Mander (London: Merlin, 1969), p. 20.

26   Ibid., p. 21. Here, Lukács employs the terminology of the German philosopher Martin Heidegger (1889–1976).

this view, and accepted a view which is called 'reflection aesthetics'. Art, for him, became then a mere reflection of social reality. It no longer had the relative autonomy which he had been able to show earlier on. Instead of seeing knowledge of society as [being as] problematic as knowledge of art, art is related to a social reality which is independently knowable. The knowledge of society is no longer problematic.

The second point which the Frankfurt School found extremely important was Lukács's stress, earlier on, on a dynamic notion of totality, and his theory of imputed class consciousness. These two notions put an emphasis on social change and contradiction. They provided the basis for a critique of the status quo and of existing consciousness. A literary criticism based on them would be able to see that social contradictions reappear in works of art, and that culture is disunited. Later on, the notion of totality which underlies Lukács's notions of bourgeois and socialist realism became a pre-given, static, and reconciled view. The concept of socialist realism presupposed that socialism had actually been achieved. Lukács fell back into the traditional concept of culture, according to which culture is seen as a unified and perfect whole.

The third point which the Frankfurt School adopted was a point taken from *The Theory of the Novel*. Lukács's *Theory of the Novel* is based on the question: Which works of art are possible in which epochs? It rests on a definition of art according to its formal qualities. For example, Lukács was asking: When does it become possible to write novels? Or lyric poetry? When can such things be understood by people? It was based on a notion of the difference between pre-capitalist, capitalist, and socialist societies. But, later on, when Lukács developed his notion of bourgeois and socialist realism, the emphasis was shifted to content, not form, and this content was defined independently of the historical epoch, as an abstract ideal. Lukács no longer stressed the differences between bourgeois and socialist realism. In the earlier work, Lukács's analysis of modern subjectivity was positive. He saw subjectivity in literature as a correlate of form, and he saw experimentations in subjectivity as innovative, subversive, and critical, and he related it to historical change. In his later work, subjectivity in literature was seen as passive, colluding, and distorting, and was accused of being ahistorical.

The first set of those points will be developed as we go along, because they were the aspects of Lukács's earlier work which were so important for subsequent Marxist aesthetics, and the second set were the points which they rejected. In subsequent weeks, we'll go on to discuss the details of Lukács's views on modernist writers, and on the relationship between modernism and society. But we'll also look at those people who considered themselves Marxists, but weren't members of the Communist Party – who used Lukács's early writings, but who supported various forms of modernism, both as artists and as theorists.

3

The Greatness and Decline of Expressionism: Ernst Bloch

Bloch is really our first Marxist modernist. He was never a member of the Frankfurt School, although he was friendly with all the major members. Like the members of the Frankfurt School, who we will be going on to discuss, Bloch was an artist as well as a Marxist, a philosopher, and a social theorist. He was as concerned to develop revolutionary art as to develop revolutionary theory. His critique of society was the foundation of the principles of innovation in his art, and vice versa: his experiments in artistic style structured the presentation of his social theory. You may remember that, in the first lecture, I said it was this addition that made the Frankfurt School interesting in the structure of the Modern European Mind course. Bloch was a writer and a musician.[1] He was closely involved with the expressionist movements in Germany before, during, and after the First World War. It has been said that the book he published in 1918, when he first became known, which was called *The Spirit of Utopia*, was the first work of expressionist social theory.[2] You may remember we

---

1   As noted in Martin Jay's afterword, Rose is probably confusing Ernst Bloch here with the American composer Ernest Bloch. While Ernst Bloch did write widely on music and musicology, he was not himself a musician or composer.

2   Ernst Bloch, *The Spirit of Utopia*, transl. Anthony A. Assar (Stanford, CA: Stanford University Press, 2000).

discussed expressionism a bit last week. I hope you remember some of the things we said about it. If you don't, I'll repeat them later on. Bloch was one of those who was very excited by Lukács's *History and Class Consciousness*, especially the analysis of reification in that book, and the possibility that the theory of reification offered for analysing new forms of domination – cultural, as well as political and economic. Bloch was also one of those who used Nietzsche's ideas in the critique of modern culture and in the development of a new concept of subjectivity. You may remember that, in the first lecture, I said that the Frankfurt School was influenced by Marx, Nietzsche, and Freud – and this is particularly true of Bloch. Like Freud, he was interested, as well, in the parapraxes of everyday life. He considered that everyday life was the clue to the formation of subjectivity and its possibilities. But, as I intimated last week, Bloch rejected Lukács's philosophy of history, he rejected Lukács's analysis of fascism, and, above all for our interests, he rejected Lukács's rejection of expressionism – Lukács's designation of expressionism and modernism in art as reactionary and decadent. In the second half of this lecture, I'm going to be comparing Lukács and Bloch on these issues. In short, Bloch was one of those who found Lukács's early work liberating, and his later work deadening. In fact, Bloch used Lukács's early ideas more consistently than Lukács himself, in his understanding of the relationship between art and society.

Who was Ernst Bloch? I'll give you a few details of his life. Like all these people, he was involved in escaping fascism and Stalinism, and lived in many different countries.[3] I'll also tell you what his major works were. He was born in 1885, in Germany, and like Lukács, who he met at university, he studied at Berlin and Heidelberg. Here he met not only Lukács, but also the sociologists Simmel and Weber. He was part of those circles. As I've said, in 1918 he wrote his first major book, called *The Spirit of Utopia*, which was largely on music. In

---

3   As Martin Jay notes in his afterword, Bloch did not 'escape' Stalinism. In fact, he was supportive of Stalin up until Khrushchev's speech to the Twentieth Party Congress in 1956, which revealed the extent of Stalin's failures. For more detail on Bloch's relationship to Stalinism and his politics more generally, see Chapter 4 in Cat Moir, *Ernst Bloch's Speculative Materialism* (Leiden: Brill, 2019), pp. 106–29.

1914–1918, he was one of the very few Germans who was opposed from the beginning to the First World War. He went into exile in Switzerland, and that was where he met Walter Benjamin, who was also in exile during that period. After the First World War, he went back to Germany, and he was very active and involved in the revolutionary movements which broke out at that period – that was between 1918 and 1923. In 1921, during this revolutionary period, he wrote another book, which subsequently became very well known, called *Thomas Münzer: Theologian of the Revolution*.[4] In fact, that's a very good description of Bloch. When it was obvious that the revolutionary movements in Germany had been defeated, Bloch was one of the first people in Germany who understood the threat of the rise of the Nazi Party. From 1924 onwards, he was trying to warn people about this. From 1933 to 1938, Bloch, like all the other members of the Frankfurt School, had to leave Germany, and he lived in Prague, Vienna, and Paris. In 1935 he published a very important book, from our point of view, which was called *Heritage of Our Times*.[5] It was a major anti-Lukács work, in which he defended expressionism and analysed fascism. He also published other articles during this period against Lukács, which appeared in Popular Front journals. In 1938, like everybody else except Lukács, he went to America, where he wrote what is known as his major work, which is being translated into English at the moment, which is called *Das Prinzip Hoffnung* (*The Principle of Hope*) – it's three gigantic volumes.[6] During this period in America, he was very close to Thomas Mann and Bertolt Brecht. With Mann and Brecht, he edited an émigré journal.[7] Bloch was one of those who, like Brecht, after the war, in 1949, went back to East Germany (not West Germany), where he was a professor at Leipzig

---

4   Ernst Bloch, *Thomas Münzer als Theologe der Revolution* (Frankfurt am Main: Suhrkamp, 1985).

5   Ernst Bloch, *Heritage of Our Times*, transl. Neville and Stephen Plaice (Cambridge: Polity, 1991).

6   Ernst Bloch, *The Principle of Hope*, 3 vols., transl. Neville Plaice, Stephen Plaice, and Paul Knight (Cambridge, MA: MIT Press, 1995).

7   As Martin Jay notes in his afterword, this is an error. Bloch was never close to Thomas Mann, and did not edit a journal with him.

University. But, in 1961, he left East Germany and went to West Germany. He stayed in West Germany, at Tübingen University, until he died – that was the summer before last, in 1977.

As I found out, some of you have already heard of Bloch. I don't know in what connection. In fact, until very recently Bloch has been best known in Germany, and especially in America, because of the enormous influence he has had on modern radical theology. Bloch is one of the few Marxist thinkers who is deeply read in both Jewish and Christian theology, and Jewish and Christian mysticism. Jürgen Moltmann, the famous theologian, wrote a book inspired by Bloch, called *Theology of Hope*, and that's one of the works that has disseminated his influence.[8] What's the connection between Marxism and theology? Let me just say, in the first instance, that Bloch, like Marx, believed that all criticism begins with a criticism of religion. But unlike Marx, Bloch didn't believe that religion is only the upholding and masking of the status quo, or only the opium of the people. Bloch believed that religion, and therefore ideology in general, can also function as what he called expressive forms of protest. He didn't merely see religion as legitimating the existing society, he thought religious movements could also be movements of revolt and protest. He was particularly interested in Christian eschatology. He was interested in Christianity as a hope for ultimate things, for what does not yet exist as the motor of history. That sounds rather cryptic – I'll be coming back to it. But this notion of the 'not yet,' the *noch nicht*, is very important to Bloch. So that's one of the reasons why Bloch has become well known: because he is one of the few Marxists who have been interested in religion.

Another preliminary question which we should ask ourselves is: In what sense is Bloch's writing – his social theory – expressionist, or modernist? Why do we call Bloch an expressionist social theorist or Marxist? His early work – it's true of his later work as well, but it's particularly true of his first book, *The Spirit of Utopia* – had several features about it which Bloch had self-consciously taken over from

---

8   Jürgen Moltmann, *Theology of Hope*, transl. J. W. Leitch (London: SCM, 2002).

expressionism: in the first place, the form and style of his work. Bloch, when he wrote, tended to juxtapose, deliberately, elements of different traditions – and this was a feature of expressionist art, too. He would juxtapose Christianity and Marxism, mysticism and social theory, in order to bring all of these things into critical focus. By use of quotation and pastiche, he tried to illuminate suppressed assumptions and raise new questions.

The second feature of his work which was associated with expressionism was his apocalyptic theory of history, and we'll be coming back to this when we contrast him with Lukács. For the moment, I will just say that Bloch rejected an evolutionary theory of history. Instead, the present became for him the Now – with a capital 'N' – that is, an absolute moment, to be analysed for the ingredients of the 'not yet': the ideal future. This apocalyptic theory of history was also associated very much with expressionist works of art. You may remember I mentioned that last week, when I gave you a brief introduction to expressionism.

The third aspect of Bloch's social theory which had a lot in common with expressionism was his emphasis on the formation and importance of subjectivity. On all aspects of subjectivity, including those aspects not considered before by either philosophy or Marxism – that is, daily life, sexuality (reactionary as well as progressive), and political positions. Now, all these interests of Bloch's were initially unified by his interest in the possibility of communist revolution in Germany. In fact, Bloch at this period, around the end of the First World War, and the period of revolution in Germany, has been called 'the German philosopher of the October Revolution'.[9] Marx said that it was Germany – that is, Kant and Hegel – who had provided the theory of the French Revolution, as a compensation for the fact that the French Revolution didn't occur in Germany – that is, there was no national

---

9   Rose takes this characterisation from Oskar Negt, 'Ernst Bloch, the German Philosopher of the October Revolution', transl. Jack Zipes, *New German Critique* 4 (Winter 1975), pp. 3–16. This essay was first printed as an afterword to Ernst Bloch's *Vom Hasard zur Katastrophe* (Frankfurt am Main: Suhrkamp, 1972).

liberal bourgeois revolution in Germany.[10] Instead, Marx said, the Germans spent all their time providing the theory of the revolution that occurred in France. Similarly, after the First World War, the German Revolution failed, but the Russian one succeeded.[11] This catchphrase describing Bloch is saying that Bloch provided the theory of the revolution which occurred in Russia and analysed why it didn't occur in Germany. In fact, it's quite true. From 1918 onwards, Bloch analysed the possibility and failure of the revolution in Germany; and from 1924 onwards he analysed the success of the reactionary revolution of fascism.

I want to say something about what Bloch took from Lukács, and where he disagreed with him. Bloch was a very close friend of Lukács's at the time he was writing *History and Class Consciousness* – that was between 1918 and 1923. In fact, he later said, wickedly, that he had written all the good bits himself. But in the 1930s he became Lukács's main antagonist in the debate over art and the rise of fascism. He

10   This may be a reference to 'Contribution to the Critique of Hegel's Philosophy of Right' (1843): 'We have shared the restorations of modern nations without ever having shared their revolutions … As the ancient peoples went through their pre-history in imagination, in *mythology*, so we Germans have gone through our post-history in thought, in *philosophy*. We are *philosophical* contemporaries of the present without being its *historical* contemporaries. German philosophy is the *ideal prolongation* of German history. If therefore, instead of the *oeuvres incomplètes* of our real history, we criticize the *oeuvres posthumes* of our ideal history, *philosophy*, our criticism is in the midst of the questions of which the present says: *That is the question*. What, in progressive nations, is a *practical* break with modern state conditions, is, in Germany, where even those conditions do not yet exist, at first a *critical* break with the philosophical reflexion of those conditions' (*MECW*, vol. 3, pp. 176, 180). Marx also makes the point more emphatically in his earlier, lesser known 'Philosophical Manifesto of the Historical School of Law' (1842): '*Kant's philosophy* must be rightly regarded as the *German theory* of the French revolution' (*MECW*, vol. 1, p. 206).

11   The Russian October Revolution of 1917 ultimately led to the creation of the Soviet Union in 1922. While the German Revolution of 1918 was successful insofar as it replaced the constitutional monarchy with a democratic parliamentary republic, it was ultimately a failure for the left. The German communist Spartacist uprising of January 1919 (led by Karl Liebknecht and Rosa Luxemburg) was crushed by the moderate Social Democratic Party in power (led by Friedrich Ebert).

became Lukács's bitterest enemy. We want to know what happened, why he changed his relationship with Lukács. We've had some discussion already on the way in which Lukács changed his own position between these two periods.

Firstly, what was Bloch excited by in *History and Class Consciousness*?[12] He was excited by some of those aspects which we discussed last week. He was excited by the analysis of reification; by Lukács's stress on the concept of totality, in the sense that Lukács emphasised totality in relationship to the loss of the old pre-capitalist one, and in relationship to the possibility of recapturing the totality as a historical ideal. He was impressed by Lukács's analysis of fragmentation in modern life, due to the technical changes in the division of labour. He was interested in Lukács's emphasis on the everyday experience of new forms of domination; but he did not accept the role that Lukács gave in the second half of *History and Class Consciousness* to the party, as the educator of the proletariat. You remember last week, we discussed the distinction Lukács makes between existing and ideal class consciousness – or imputed class consciousness, which is what Lukács called it. In fact, although we didn't discuss it last week, in the second half of *History and Class Consciousness*, Lukács gives a central role to the communist party as the means by which the transition will be made from existing class consciousness to imputed or ideal class consciousness. It was this part of his analysis which Bloch was most seriously opposed to, and so were the rest of the Frankfurt School. Since he rejected this idea of the party as the educator of the proletariat, he also rejected Lukács's theory of history on which that role of the party is based. He believed that Lukács had reduced history to a single dimension with a linear structure – that is, the proletariat's path from reified to imputed or ideal class consciousness, with the party as its guide.

Instead of this gradualist theory in which reification is progressively overcome, Bloch draws the equally logical conclusion that

12   For more, see Bloch's review of *History and Class Consciousness*: 'Actuality and Utopia: On Lukács' *History and Class Consciousness*' (1923), transl. Cat Moir, *Thesis Eleven* 157: 1 (2020), pp. 3–23.

reification will have to be exploded. There's no guarantee that it will melt away. He emphasises the present or the Now as having the utopian possibilities within it. Unlike Lukács, he does not project the ideal society into the historical future; he stresses instead the moment of decision, that revolution is a qualitative leap, not a gradual or guided achievement. Existing class consciousness, according to Bloch, is not working towards ideal class consciousness, but already possesses it in suppressed forms: in art, in fantasies, in ideologies. But Bloch's view is not voluntaristic – he's not saying that revolution simply depends on an act of will. His view is, in fact, based on a historical account of the present which does not stress the present as a culmination of the past, or as a superseding of the past, but instead stresses the various ways in which the different pasts still live in the present and may be realised within it. Bloch substitutes his own notion of the sphere of the present in place of Lukács's notion of the totality of history. Bloch's notion of the sphere emphasises a structure, rather than a process. He called the sphere 'the expression of different subject–object levels in the process itself'.[13] By 'subject–object levels', Bloch meant that, at any point in time, there are many different classes in a society, each with their class consciousness at different stages from the actual to the ideal – that's Lukács's distinction again. Therefore, he differed from Lukács in believing that, for a successful revolution, it is necessary to transform all classes, not just the proletariat; and secondly, he believed that actual as opposed to ideal class consciousness must not be considered merely as false consciousness or delusion, as many Marxists tended to do. He quoted Lukács against Lukács. Lukács said, 'we must discover . . . the *practical* significance of these different possible relations between the objective economic totality, imputed class consciousness, and the real, psychological thoughts of men about their lives'; but Bloch said that Lukács didn't pay enough attention to the real, psychological thoughts of men, and their lives.[14]

Why did Bloch turn so much away from Lukács? It was because he

---

13   Ibid., p. 20.
14   Georg Lukács, *History and Class Consciousness: Studies in Marxist Dialectics*, transl. Rodney Livingstone (London: Merlin, 2010), p. 51. Emphasis in original.

linked the faults in Lukács's *History and Class Consciousness* to the success of fascism. He believed that the defeat of the working class in the '20s was linked to the defects of socialist and communist theory, and that, vice versa, these reasons for the defeat of the working class and the defects of Marxist theory were equally the reasons for the success of fascism. How did Bloch explain this, or make this link? It depended on a reinterpretation of the classic Marxist theory of social change.[15] The classic Marxist view of social change is that social change occurs when new forces of production come into contradiction with old, existing relations of production. A contradiction then develops in two senses. There's a contradiction between the old ruling class and the new ruling class – for example, in the transition from feudalism to capitalism between the land-owning aristocracy and the entrepreneurial bourgeoisie. And, as the new social relations develop, a second contradiction appears between the bourgeoisie and the working class, for the bourgeoisie's existence is based on the appropriation of private profit, while the working class's existence is based on socialised labour. Now this contradiction, which is a classic one, the developing contradiction between the bourgeoisie and the working class, Bloch called a contemporaneous contradiction – that is, the fundamental basic contradiction of capitalism. He called it 'contemporaneous' – I'm afraid it's a dreadful word, but it's the best translation of it that I can think of.[16] But Bloch emphasised that the capitalist mode of production also inherits contradictions from other earlier modes of production, which do not merely survive within the new mode of production but are actually reproduced by it. This, in fact, is what Marx called the theory of the uneven development of capitalism.[17] This theory states

---

15   This reinterpretation is found primarily in *Erbschaft dieser Zeit* (*Heritage of Our Times*). The key passage which Rose goes on to explicate is translated and reproduced as Ernst Bloch, 'Nonsynchronism and the Obligation to Its Dialectics', transl. Mark Ritter, *New German Critique* 11 (Spring 1977), pp. 22–38.

16   The standard translation of this word (*gleichzeitig*) in Marxist scholarship has since been 'simultaneous', or else 'synchronous'.

17   While the concept of combined and uneven development is certainly latent in Marx, it was only fully developed by Leon Trotsky. See in particular Leon Trotksy, *The Third International after Lenin* (1928), transl. John G. Wright (New York: Pathfinder, 1970).

that the development of capitalism depends on pockets of pre-capitalist activity which can be destroyed, incorporated, or perpetuated,
depending on the needs of the dominant capitalist system. Bloch
called this secondary network of contradictions 'non-contemporaneous [*ungleichzeitig*] contradictions'. So, Bloch made the distinction
between two kinds of contradictions between social classes in
advanced capitalist society: the fundamental contradiction, which
Marx pointed to, between the bourgeoisie and the proletariat, which
he called a 'contemporaneous contradiction'; and other contradictions
between the dominant capitalist classes and those classes which had
survived from other modes of production – and not merely survived,
but whose existence was perpetuated by capitalism. He called this
'non-contemporaneous' because they were classes inherited or reproduced from an earlier period; and he called it a 'contradiction' because
he believed that these classes would also be in revolt against capitalist
society. They were also potentially revolutionary classes; but their
potentially revolutionary force would usually be reactionary.

What were these groups or classes? Bloch was interested in three
particularly. The first one is the young, or youth. He thought that this
group, although they were likely to be opposed to the existing society,
were potentially the most progressive group, for they exist with a
sense of the incompletion of their society. They are filled with dreams,
and they take their strength from the possible future; they tend to be
utopian. The other two classes tend to be reactionary. The first of
these is the peasantry: a class inherited from a previous mode of
production but reproduced within the capitalist system. This was
particularly true of Germany, where capitalist social relations tended
not to penetrate the countryside. The peasantry still possessed the
means of production and lived a fairly stable communal existence,
unlike capitalist classes. However, they tended to be anti-capitalist
and politically regressive. The third class is the petite bourgeoisie, and
was divided into two: the old petite bourgeoisie, and the new petite
bourgeoisie. The old petite bourgeoisie – that is, those who were self-
employed – had become impoverished, and for this reason they
tended to be opposed to advanced capitalist society. The new petite
bourgeoisie was salaried workers and bureaucrats: people who were

not direct producers, like the proletariat, but whose conditions of work had often been proletarianised. These two groups of the petite bourgeoisie, Bloch also thought, would be potentially anti-capitalist. He said that they develop what he called an 'alogical space in which wishes and romanticisms, primal drives, and mysticisms come onto the stage'.[18] These are the three groups, inherited from previous modes of production, which would yet be in revolt against capitalist society.

He thought that it was very important to analyse the subjective aspects of their political experience. He drew on Nietzsche to do this. He drew on Nietzsche's distinction between Apollo and Dionysus in his rephrasing of Lukács's theory of reification.[19] He called Apollo what Lukács called reification – that is, the cold, unfeeling rationality of a reified society in which people cannot understand what's going on, but against which they revolt. The principle of Dionysus he used to stress the emotional or subjective side of people's experience, as expressed in dreams, fantasies, and ideology. He thought that this side of people's lives, in a society in which the social process was basically incomprehensible to them, would be susceptible to illusions and ideologies, even those which are against their own interests. But he didn't just have a negative view of this susceptibility to ideology and illusion. He thought that their acceptance of such illusions was always an expression of a human potential which nourishes itself with illusion only insofar as it cannot find expression in reality. He had a very positive interpretation of illusions and ideologies. Bloch considered the twentieth century as having special possibilities for revolutionary change due to the eclipse of religion, because the turn away from otherworldly salvations to social existence had returned to men the unfilled potentialities of the present. Utopia, for Bloch, is located in concrete existence, in everyday objects, in bohemian life, in expressionism or modernism, in art, and in music. Utopia, for Bloch, is, as it were, a cultural surplus – in the world, but not of it.

---

18   Bloch, 'Nonsynchronism and the Obligation to Its Dialectics', p. 26.
19   See in particular Bloch, *The Principle of Hope*, vol. 3; and Nietzsche, *The Birth of Tragedy*, transl. Ronald Spiers, ed. Raymond Geuss and Ronald Spiers (Cambridge: Cambridge University Press, 2004).

The crucial thing is that he linked this to the success of fascism. He believed that it was the fascists, and not the left, who had given political form to modern utopian substance, to this cultural surplus. In doing so, fascism or Nazism had depoliticised this substance. Bloch was one of the only Marxists who took seriously the power of fascism as a cultural synthesis. It was those groups which I've already mentioned – the young, the peasantry, and the petite bourgeoisie – with their specific political grievances, that fascism had appealed to. Fascism, unlike the left, had been able to appeal to the regressive and repressed forms in which the grievances of these groups expressed themselves. Bloch accused the left of having ignored these groups as merely reactionary. Instead, he argued that a successful proletarian revolution, while it must be based on the fundamental contemporaneous contradiction, can only ignore the non-contemporaneous contradictions at its peril. It must instead enlist the previous contradictions – it must animate and awaken their critical and utopian potential. It must change their particular political resentment and regressions into what is potentially progressive and universal in the struggle of the proletariat. It should detach these classes from their dreams and images of a better past [and move them towards] images of a better future. Bloch called this 'multi-level dialectics'.[20] That's, of course, a polemical criticism of Lukács, whose dialectics he considered to be unilinear and monolithic. These are all the things that he thought the left had failed to do. Instead, fascism had stepped in, and had obtained a monopoly of appeal to the mystical and romantic anti-capitalism of these three classes. It had channelled the merely archaic and irrational aspects of their experience, while the left had neglected what Bloch wanted to call 'revolutionary fantasy'. The left had seen fascist ideology as a mere form of deception, instead of decoding it as a form of wish-fulfilment. Fascism – which would cover any sort of reactionary political movement or ideology – according to Bloch, represents a distorted and inverted hope, what he called a 'swindle of fulfilment'.[21]

---

20   Bloch, 'Nonsynchronism and the Obligation to Its Dialectics', pp. 35–6.

21   Quoted in Anson Rabinbach, 'Unclaimed Heritage: Ernst Bloch's *Heritage of Our Times* and the Theory of Fascism', *New German Critique* 11 (Spring 1977), pp. 5–21.

It was these views on the relationship between political experience and imagery which structured Bloch's dispute with Lukács over expressionism. You may remember last week I discussed Lukács's criticism of expressionism and *Proletkult*, and how, ultimately, in the work he wrote in 1956, *The Meaning of Contemporary Realism*, he had lumped together all the many different forms of modernism into one thing, which he contrasted with realism. We looked in very general terms at what his criticisms were of modernist works of art. Now, I'm going to be a bit more specific, and tell you what were Lukács's specific arguments against expressionism. It was these arguments against expressionism which lay behind the more general views against modernism, although Lukács, at this point, isn't really considering *Proletkult* as much. Somebody actually came up to me at the end of last week's lecture and asked what exactly Lukács did say about the relationship between fascism and expressionism. It is quite true that I didn't go into it, although I did mention that Lukács equated the two. This week I'll try and show you how he linked them.

Lukács and the other members of the German Communist Party who went to Moscow associated fascism with all forms of irrationalism in bourgeois culture. They saw fascist ideology as an expression of the decline and decadence of bourgeois culture. They considered that expressionist art was a symptom of the same decline. Instead of combating that decline, expressionist art had colluded in it. Lukács refused to see expressionism as itself a form of criticism of bourgeois society, as progressive or revolutionary in any sense at all. He thought that expressionist distortion – that is, distortion in expressionist works of art – was merely a mirror-image of a distorted society, rather than an attempt to understand and analyse social reality, or an attempt which tried to shock people out of their usual perceptions of that reality. Lukács simply equated the decline of society with the decline of art, which he saw as homogeneous and linear. Dissolution in art has no positive potential at all, no utopian aspects. He thought that the representation of dissolution in art was a false solution – pacifist and escapist. Instead, Lukács believed that art, by which he understood classical and realist art, should develop a mediated knowledge of the totality – that is, it should not be based on the presentation of

immediate experience, but should attempt to understand that immediate experience by relating it to an understanding of the whole society. Expressionist art, on the contrary, he believed, was solipsistic and
idiosyncratic, a revolt of the petite bourgeoisie which obscures social
reality, instead of illuminating it, by merely reproducing its surface
features, and not relating those surface features to the larger underlying processes. Lukács accused Bloch of contributing to all of these
ills, of doing as a theorist exactly what expressionists were doing in
art – which of course, as I've said, is what Bloch was self-consciously
desiring to do.

Bloch opposed Lukács on all these issues. (From now, when I use
the word 'expressionism' you should take it as well to mean 'modernism'). Expressionism for Bloch meant the search for new artistic
forms to represent new forms of experience. This art seeks out and
presents the revolutionary tensions and possibilities in a society. It
is a more or less explicit oppositional art. He disliked and rejected
Lukács's designation of the times as decadent. He thought that
designation was static and ahistorical. It is necessary for the artist,
as well as the theorist, always to see the contradictions and possibilities in the present. All times, said Bloch, are dialectical – that is,
contradictory, transitory, and containing the future. Lukács's view
was the defeatist one. Expressionist art tries to capture this, to illuminate the social possibilities. Bloch accused Lukács of despising
the present, and of not writing or understanding it as an artist, or
considering individual works of art. He pointed out that the fascists,
too, denounced expressionism, and that it was rather paradoxical
that Lukács should too, since he was so opposed to fascism. He
believed that Lukács had denied in principle the possibility of any
genuine artistic innovation, of any avant-garde in late-capitalist
society. He got his own back on Lukács by showing how Lukács
idealised classical art; how Lukács refused to analyse its class
connections; that one might argue that the art which Lukács idealised – that is, the realist art of the early bourgeois period – could
also be shown to be passive and escapist. In fact, Lukács is glorify-
ing early bourgeois art, because he sees it as the art of the not-yet-
disintegrated society. Lukács, in short, assumes a closed and

integrated totality. He does not see that expressionism has tried to challenge that totality.

To sum up their differences, Lukács is, in fact, assuming continuity in history, whilst Bloch assumes discontinuity. What Lukács sees as collusion with decadence, Bloch was able to see as art taking over the active and positive elements in society. Even if it's true that modern society was in decay, Bloch would say that growth comes from decay. Lukács, also, was wrong to deny that expressionist art had any links with the past. In fact, expressionist poets and artists were very conscious of their link with previous periods of critical art. Bloch, in fact, claimed that expressionist art was a breakthrough to popular art, because it appealed to the potentially revolutionary emotions, to the subjective side of people's experience, whereas Lukács's ideal of art was abstract and rejected anything which could not be simply labelled proletarian or bourgeois realism. Of course, Bloch was delighted that Lukács accused him of doing in his theory what he was doing in his art, because that's what he believed one had to do.

In conclusion, I would just like to ask: Who was right? We have two conflicting positions here on a whole range of issues concerning the relationship between art and society. Admittedly, it's at a specific point in time, but, as I've tried to bring out in the last few lectures, these debates over expressionism and fascism still structure the debates of the relationship between modernist art and society that we are interested in today. Believe it or not, after all this, I think that both Lukács and Bloch are wrong. Paradoxically, I think they're wrong for the same reasons. There are three ways in which I think this is true.

If you think about it, Bloch is developing his arguments from the point of view of the artist, of the composition or production of works of art, whereas Lukács is considering expressionist or modernist art from the point of view of their reception, of their effect or social function. Bloch makes the assumption, it seems to me, that art is always received as it is intended, whereas Lukács makes the assumption that art is always intended as it has been received. Now, considering that both of them were so interested in reification – that is, the extension of commodity relations to other areas of life – it seems to me that they both overlooked something. They overlooked the fact that in a society in which art is transformed into commodities, it's quite possible for intervening processes to come in between the production and reception of works of art, and to distort their original significance. If we take this into account, then it could be that Bloch is right to the extent that his position represents how expressionist and modernist art *hopes* to relate to society, whereas Lukács could be [right to the extent that his position represents how expressionist and modernist art actually relates to society, i.e. that it failed to have this desired effect. If that is true, we can say][22] that they both exaggerated one view because neither of them considered that, in a society in which works of art become commodities, it's impossible just to consider works of art according to either the artistic intention or how they are received. There may be a contradiction between the process of composing a work of art and its social reception. If you find this idea a bit strange, I'll be talking about that more when I come onto Adorno.

The second sense in which they both share assumptions – in which I think these assumptions are very dubious – is this: Bloch says, and it is an attractive position, that art, and political movements as well, can, and should, and must draw on and appeal to the emotional and the irrational. Otherwise, it will leave these aspects of human experience to the enemy. Lukács hated Bloch's position. He thought it was a dangerous and false emphasis – that it was an appeal to the irrational aspects of thought and of experience. It seems to me that, on this issue, they were both wrong. Bloch was wrong to see the emotional or the irrational as universal and fundamental. In fact, what counts as emotional or subjective in a society is produced and reproduced by the social structure. Whereas Lukács was wrong because he had far too rigid a definition of what will count as realistic or rational at any point in time. He was wrong for the same reason, for he saw what is realistic or what is rational as universal, pre-given, and fixed.

Finally, it seems they were both wrong in another assumption which they accepted, and that was the idea that, between 1918 and 1950, bourgeois culture was in dissolution or disintegration. Lukács,

---

22   The recording cuts out for nine seconds. The contents of the square brackets are interpolated by the editors.

as you know, saw this as a period heralding the end of culture. Bloch wasn't quite so pessimistic, but he certainly saw this period of dissolution as a period of transition. Neither of them considered that, in fact, it might be a period in which bourgeois society, or late-capitalist society, was consolidating itself – consolidating new modes of domination – and that it wasn't a period of dissolution at all. This was the conclusion of the rest of the Frankfurt School. They too, like Bloch, based this conclusion on the notion of discontinuity in history. Both Bloch and Lukács, it seems to me, were wrong in the third instance in assuming that that period was a period of dissolution or decadence or decay. The later Frankfurt School, especially in this book *Dialectic of Enlightenment*, pointed out how, in fact, the importance of this period was the development of new forms of cultural and political domination.

Nevertheless, I think if I had to choose, although don't quote me on it, I would take Bloch's view of history and art as the more open-minded and flexible, as the more likely to produce an effective and non-authoritarian cultural politics.

Next week I'll be talking about Walter Benjamin.

4

The Battle over Walter Benjamin

Benjamin is our second Marxist modernist. Bloch, last week, was the first one. In Benjamin's work, art and theory are even more insepara- ble than they were in the case of Ernst Bloch. Benjamin composed his social theory with a rare stylistic perfectionism. If he wrote about Baroque art, his texts became a Baroque masterpiece; if he wrote about Romantic irony, his texts became Romantic and ironic. Like Lukács, Bloch, and many other members of the Frankfurt School, Benjamin's work was radical and sociological before he was influ- enced by Marxism. Like Bloch, after he was influenced by Marxism, he continued to be impressed by Lukács's early pre-Marxist work, especially Lukács's work on the relationship between artistic form and historical change, and the reification thesis of *History and Class Consciousness*; but, also like Bloch and the rest of the Frankfurt School, he rejected Lukács's later work on bourgeois and socialist realism.

This lecture is divided into two halves; but, unlike the other lectures, in the first half I am going to discuss some of Benjamin's central ideas, and only in the second half am I going to ask the ques- tion: Who was Walter Benjamin? In the first half, I'm going to discuss Benjamin's attempt to develop a Marxist concept of experience (I'll explain what I mean by that); his attempt to write a Marxist history of modernity; his theory of the relationship between different modes of production and works of art; and his theses on history and the proletariat. In the second half of the lecture, I'm going to ask: Who was Walter Benjamin? The reason for this is because I want to say something about the reception of Benjamin in the English- and American-speaking world. I want to introduce you to some of the controversies over his work. I suppose the most important thing that you ought to know about this is that Benjamin committed suicide in 1940, which was very early. He was very young – forty-eight, I think, at the time. Benjamin since then has become an essentially contested author. The fight over his heritage brings together some of the central disputes over philosophy, Marxist theory, and aesthetics – and it is still continuing.

I want to just outline Benjamin's major works. I'll go through that outline in a minute, but one of the first things I'd like to point out to you is that in Benjamin's lifetime he published only 550 printed pages. He only published two books. The first one was the one on German Romanticism, which was his doctoral thesis, and the other one was *The Origin of German Tragic Drama*.[1] All the rest of the things he published were essays and reviews – he wrote a lot of book reviews. He was never an academic philosopher. His collected works, which are being published at the moment in German, are not complete, because a lot of Benjamin's manuscripts were destroyed by the Nazis, and an enormous number of manuscripts are in East Germany, in an archive in Potsdam, outside Berlin, and the East Germans won't let anybody near them.[2] So, there are thousands of Benjamin manuscripts which we don't even have. Apart from that, in the collected works, 5,000 sides are being published.[3] Benjamin himself only

---

1   Walter Benjamin, 'The Concept of Criticism in German Romanticism', transl. David Lachterman, Howard Eiland, and Ian Balfour, in *Walter Benjamin: Selected Writings*, vol. 1, *1913–1926*, ed. Marcus Bullock and Michael W. Jennings (Cambridge, MA: Belknap, 1999), pp. 116–200; Walter Benjamin, *The Origin of German Tragic Drama*, transl. John Osborne (London: Verso, 2009).

2   The Walter Benjamin Archive is now housed in Luisenstrasse, Berlin.

3   Walter Benjamin, *Gesammelte Schriften*, 7 vols, ed. Rolf Tiedemann and Hermann Schweppenhäuser (Frankfurt am Main: Suhrkamp, 1972–99).

published 550, and his collected [works], which are not complete, consist of over 5,000. You might begin to see why the reception of Benjamin has taken quite a long time to get going.

Benjamin's major works consist of his doctoral thesis on German Romanticism, which he published in 1920; and a short study – it's not book-length – of Goethe's novel *Elective Affinities* (I don't know if you know *Elective Affinities* – it is available in English translation, although not Benjamin's commentary on it).[4] Neither of those two early works are available in English, and as far as I know there are no plans to translate them, which is a pity.[5] His major pre-Marxist work, *The Origin of German Tragic Drama*, is available in English translation, and he published that in 1928. That was his second dissertation. In Germany you have to do two doctorates in order to have a tenured academic job. In fact, that second dissertation of Benjamin's was rejected by the faculty at Frankfurt University, with the result that he was never able to get an academic job.[6] Because of that, he spent the rest of his life, from 1928 until 1940, as a freelance writer, journalist, and so on. But he did work on two major projects. One is what I've called *Paris; or Baudelaire*, his work on France at the beginning of the nineteenth century.[7] Very, very little of it was published during his lifetime, but selections of it have since been published under the heading *Charles Baudelaire* – it's on the reading list, I think.[8] Then there's a series of articles on Brecht.[9] He also published many essays,

---

4 Walter Benjamin, 'Goethe's Elective Affinities', in *Selected Writings*, vol. 1, pp. 297–360. Johann Wolfgang von Goethe, *Elective Affinities*, transl. David Constantine (Oxford: Oxford University Press, 2008).

5 As noted above, they are both now available in English.

6 Benjamin finished the work in 1925, but the faculty, including Max Horkheimer, found it impenetrable. They therefore suggested that he withdraw it from consideration. See Esther Leslie, *Walter Benjamin* (London: Reaktion, 2007), p. 67.

7 Rose is referring here to Walter Benjamin, *The Arcades Project*, ed. Rolf Tiedemann, transl. Howard Eiland and Kevin McLaughlin (Cambridge, MA: Belknap, 2002).

8 Walter Benjamin, *Charles Baudelaire: A Lyric Poet in the Era of High Capitalism*, transl. Harry Zohn (London: Verso, 1997).

9 These articles are collected in Walter Benjamin, *Understanding Brecht*, transl. Anna Bostock (London: Verso, 2003).

one of which is quite famous, called 'The Work of Art in the Age of Mechanical Reproduction'.[10] That's available in the English volume called *Illuminations*. Just before he died, in 1940, he published his 'Theses on the Philosophy of History'.[11] They're also in that book, *Illuminations*. That's the outline of his work. It's very fragmentary.

Benjamin was interested in precisely those periods of literary history and works of art which Lukács was not interested in. For the later Lukács, the paradigm of a successful, socially committed, and responsible art was classic realist art – that is, the total, rounded, harmonious, autonomous work. When art did not conform to this paradigm, Lukács interpreted it as the period and art of social decline and disintegration. You may remember that from the earlier lecture on Lukács. For Benjamin, on the contrary, there was no such thing as classic art. The concept of the artwork, for him, was always problematic in its relationship to society and in itself. He was interested in those periods and art forms where the ambiguity of the status of a work of art in relationship to the society which had produced it was most evident. He was interested, for example, in the German seventeenth-century Baroque; in late eighteenth-century and early nineteenth-century German Romanticism; and in twentieth-century expressionism and Surrealism – especially the authors Proust, Kafka, and Brecht. Benjamin believed that more could be learnt about the relationship between artistic form and sociohistorical change not from the typical, average, or classic work, but, on the contrary, by looking at the untypical, at what he called 'the distant extremes', 'the apparent excesses of development'; by comparing antithetical exemplars of artworks.[12]

---

10   Walter Benjamin, 'The Work of Art in the Age of Mechanical Reproduction', in *Illuminations*, ed. Hannah Arendt, transl. Harry Zohn (New York: Schocken, 2007), pp. 217–52. As Martin Jay notes, the theses were actually published posthumously.

11   Walter Benjamin, 'Theses on the Philosophy of History', in *Illuminations*, pp. 253–64.

12   This is Rose's translation. Osborne's translation reads: 'Philosophical history, the science of the origin, is the form which, in the remotest extremes and the apparent excesses of the process of development, reveals the configuration of the idea – the sum total of all possible meaningful juxtapositions of such opposites.' Benjamin, *Origin of German Tragic Drama*, p. 47.

Now, I said that he was interested in developing a Marxist concept of modern experience. That, you may remember, links up with the emphasis I've put on one of the themes of this course of lectures: that the Frankfurt School are Marxist modernists interested in developing a new concept of subjectivity. By 'experience', it is not meant the empiricist sense of experience, but what I would call a dialectical notion of experience, in the sense of – I'm going to give you a German word which is not quite translatable into English – what's called *Bildung*. *Bildung* means formation, education, or culture; and experience in the sense of *Bildung* is a process which starts from the observation and partial understanding of aspects of everyday social life, and leads in stages of increasing self-knowledge to a grasp of the totality. You may recognise that as quite similar to what Benjamin understood by totality. In fact, Benjamin ultimately wanted to deny that this kind of experience was any longer possible; but first of all he wanted to capture the moments at which he thought it was still possible. By [the phrase] modern experience, he was interested in capturing and recapitulating those moments when a new form of life – and a new form of life was especially associated, for Benjamin, with technological change – occurs for the first time. We cannot assimilate it to what is old and familiar. Benjamin developed a theory of what he called 'shocks' to designate such occasions. Much of his later work consists of evoking these moments of new experience.

Now, I've said that Benjamin was interested in developing a Marxist concept of modern experience, but in previous lectures I've stressed that we mustn't use this word 'modern' to cover what are really many different movements. Benjamin himself used 'modern' in a sense which we haven't actually encountered, which was one of its original meanings, and that is dating it from the beginning of the nineteenth century – that is, not using 'modern' to refer indiscriminately to anything post-Renaissance, nor using it simply in the sense of 'contemporary'. The modern, for Benjamin, was to be dated from the beginning of the nineteenth century, and that is quite a standard use. Benjamin, like Lukács, tended to use 'modern' to cover several different movements, but for exactly the opposite reason to Lukács. You may remember that I said that Lukács used

the word 'modern' because he wanted to lump under it expressionism, *Proletkult*, and Surrealism. Benjamin, too, wanted to use the
word 'modern' to cover features of expressionism, *Proletkult*, and
Surrealism; but, unlike Lukács, he did so in a positive way, not a
negative way. The epitome of the modern for Benjamin was the
history of Paris in the nineteenth century, and his major work was
called *Paris, Capital of the Nineteenth Century*.[13] This was partly
because of all the revolutions which occurred in Paris in the nineteenth century, and because of its being a central point of artistic
and cultural activity in France. Benjamin also wrote a lot of what I
would call sociological autobiographical writings, and a volume of
these has recently been translated into English – the volume that's
called *Reflections*, on the reading list.[14] He wrote two important
autobiographical pieces. One was called *Berlin Childhood around
1900*, in which he discussed his own childhood somewhat in the
manner of Proust;[15] and another book called *One-Way Street*, which
was a discussion of living in Berlin during the Depression of the late
1920s.[16] When Benjamin was analysing these new forms of experience, he didn't limit his examination to the experience of any
particular social class; nor did he say, like Lukács, that any particular class would be privileged in understanding these experiences.
But, like Bloch, the possibility of proletarian revolution, for

---

13   This was Benjamin's working title for *The Arcades Project*, which is probably
what Rose is referring to here. However, there also exist two versions of an essay with
this same title, 'Paris, Hauptstadt des XIX Jahrhunderts'. See 'Paris, the Capital of the
Nineteenth Century' (1935), in *The Arcades Project*, pp. 3–13, and 'Paris, Capital of
the Nineteenth Century' (1939), in *The Arcades Project*, pp. 14–26.

14   Walter Benjamin, *Reflections: Essays, Aphorisms, Autobiographical Writings*,
ed. Peter Demetz, transl. Edmund Jephcott (Boston: Mariner, 2019).

15   *Berliner Kindheit um 1900* has a complicated publication history. First
written in 1932, but substantially rewritten in 1938, it was first published
posthumously in 1950. A later version in 1972 included material that had been left
out of the 1950 edition. In 1982 (after Rose's lectures), a full version was discovered,
arranged by Benjamin himself. This was published in 1989 in the *Gesammelte
Schriften*, and translated into English in 2002 in volume 3 of the *Selected Writings*, pp.
344–413.

16   Walter Benjamin, 'One-Way Street', in *Selected Writings*, vol. 1, pp. 444–88.

Benjamin, depended on a rupture in history, not on a gradual process of evolution.

Benjamin's own modernism is split into two different kinds. On the one hand, he was interested in the kind of modernism which consisted in the parody of old forms: in the use of pastiche, quotation, montage, documentation; in juxtaposing various scraps of history as a way of examining the possibilities of the present. On the other hand, he was interested in another kind of modernism, which abandoned all the old forms as implicated in the old society and tried to create a wholly changed artistic form. This ideal rested on the notion of purifying language and particularly, in the case of Benjamin, of a new technological art which would dictate its own reception. I'll come back to that idea, but you need to grasp this distinction between a modernism which is interested in parodying old forms, in comparing them with each other as a way of breaking out of them, and a kind of modernism which was interested in creating a wholly different kind of art.

The first work of Benjamin's which I want to talk about is the work which has been translated into English under the title *The Origin of German Tragic Drama*. That's a seriously misleading title, because the German word for 'tragic drama' is *Trauerspiel*, which doesn't mean 'tragic' at all. It means 'mourning play', or 'funereal pageant'.[17] Benjamin was trying precisely to illuminate a form of drama which wasn't tragic in the classical sense. You may notice that the title of this work, *The Origin of German Tragic Drama*, is an allusion to Nietzsche's book, *The Birth of Tragedy*. This allusion was intended by Benjamin. He had the same aim as Nietzsche in his book *The Birth of Tragedy*. Nietzsche, in *The Birth of Tragedy*, rejected a traditional view of German classicism, that Greek art, especially Greek tragedy, was the moral representation of a perfect, happy, harmonious society. Instead,

---

17   The German word *Tragödid* is usually held to be equivalent with the German word *Trauerspiel*. Rose is playing on the etymology of *Trauerspiel*, which is formed from the verb *trauern*, 'to mourn', and *Spiel*, 'play or drama'. The idea of a 'mourning play' or 'funereal pageant' is a technical term and a neologism, whereas *Trauerspiel* is an ordinary German word.

Nietzsche understood tragedy as a violent, nihilistic, cultic dithyramb; as an ecstatic, wild, outpouring; what he called Dionysus;
which was tamed by the illusions or discipline of form: Apollo.[18]
Benjamin, similarly, wanted to show, in opposition to Lukács's notion
of the classic, perfect work, that German seventeenth-century
Baroque tragedy – or, as I've suggested, what should be called 'mourning pageant' – appears to be the presentation of historical events, a
secular drama concerned with regal and political history; but under
examination, the emblems and objects of that drama – ruins, relics,
death's heads – are seen to have an allegorical significance. The artistic form of *Trauerspiel* – that is, funereal pageant – is seen to present
a society deeply disturbed in its relation to the natural world, the
world of nature and of history. This world becomes, in the plays, a
process of corruption – an allegory of the fall of man.

This notion of a society which has produced an art in which objects
have taken on a significance of their own, cut off from human intentionality, which are then seen as an allegory of man's fall from grace,
is the basis of Benjamin's interpretation of modern commodity-
producing society too. You may remember from our discussion of
reification, which I'll be going back over, that this notion of allegory,
the notion of a society in which objects have become cut off from
human practice and have obtained a life of their own, has some similarities with the notion of commodity fetishism. I'll be bringing them
up later on, but the interesting thing is that Benjamin had this interpretation before he had read Marx.

When Benjamin later discovered Lukács's work and read Marx, he
developed a sociology of the relationship between art forms and
different kinds of societies. This sociology, like Bloch's work, and like
the rest of the Frankfurt School, depends on Lukács's generalising of
Marx's theory of commodity fetishism. But Benjamin did it in [such]
a way [as] to oppose Lukács's view of culture. You may remember
that, for Lukács, the possibility of culture depends on organic unity in
a society, and that culture is destroyed in a society when works of art

18   A 'dithyramb' is a wild or impassioned Ancient Greek choral hymn, often
dedicated to the god Dionysus.

are turned into commodities. Benjamin, on the contrary, wanted to show that what we call autonomy in art is in fact only achieved under capitalism – it actually depends on the commodity form. He also wanted to show, in opposition to Lukács, that this autonomy or culture depends, not on organic unity, but precisely on contradictions in a society.

Benjamin distinguishes three different kinds of society. The first one is a ritualistic or primitive society; the second one is what he calls 'high capitalism'; and the third one is the society of mechanical reproduction.[19]

In the first kind of society – a ritualistic or primitive society – art is 'cult'. The work of art is continuous with other forms of social practice. Works of art are ceremonial objects designed to serve in a cult, in an immediate context of use and ritual. They have an 'aura' of magical efficacy.

Under capitalism, when art objects are exchanged as commodities, works of art become detached from an immediate context of use and ritual, and acquire a value in exchange. They become objects for exhibition, separate from other forms of social practice. They thereby acquire a semblance of autonomy. They are considered unique, and thus impart a certain aura which is retained from the authority of their tradition, and from their apparent separation from a social base. In this particular relationship, Benjamin is trying to show that what we understand by autonomy precisely depends on a certain sort of social determination.

In the third period, artworks are mechanically reproduced. Benjamin was thinking particularly of the development of photography and film. As a result of their mechanical reproduction, their aura is destroyed. Their aura of magical efficacy in a primitive society, and their aura of uniqueness and autonomy in a capitalist society – this aura is now destroyed. The works no longer seem permanent and unique. They are detached from tradition by the new technology. This new technology also destroys their semblance of autonomy, for

---

19   In the following passage, Rose provides an overview of Benjamin's essay, 'The Work of Art in the Age of Mechanical Reproduction.'

the relation of art to the forces of production in a society becomes clear. Benjamin believed that this clear relationship of art to the forces of production would help the masses to emancipate themselves from the tradition and authority of the classical work. Benjamin also emphasised that the development of mechanical reproduction would mean that works of art were increasingly composed or produced for mechanical reproducibility, and that this too would destroy the illusions of art's autonomy and ambiguity. It would completely change the social function of art, which could now become instrumental for specific political ends. Here, in fact, Benjamin was applying the ideas of *Proletkult* to the conditions of an advanced capitalist society. You may remember our discussion of *Proletkult* in the lecture on Lukács.

In Benjamin's history of modernity, he devoted himself to analysing the second and third kinds of society which we just mentioned: art in the era of high capitalism, and art in the era of mechanical reproduction. In his work on Paris, as the capital of the nineteenth century, he developed his own use of the concept of reification. You will remember that the concept of reification was central to Lukács's generalising of the theory of commodity fetishism to analyse new forms of domination. Benjamin also centred his analysis on an understanding of the concept of reification, but he modified it in his own way in order to be able to analyse the allegories of a commodity-producing society. He emphasised the idea that commodities, when they become detached from production, take on a life of their own. You may remember the classic phrase from Marx on commodity fetishism, which I quoted in a previous lecture, and which I'm now going to repeat: 'A definite social relation between men assumes the phantasmagoric form of a relation between things.'[20]

We have seen how Lukács and Bloch based on this idea (of a social structure which is systematically misunderstood) their analysis of new forms of cultural domination. Benjamin took off a different aspect of Marx's account: the idea that commodities take on a personified, phantasmagoric life of their own. 'Phantasmagoria' means a crowd or succession of dim or doubtfully real persons – that's the

---

20   Marx, *Capital*, vol. 1, p. 165. Rose's translation.

dictionary definition.[21] Benjamin believed that the social types typical of a capitalist society were also determined by the extension of the commodity form. He took the phantasmagoria of high capitalism from the motifs of Baudelaire's poems, especially the section called 'Scenes from Parisian Life' ['Tableaux Parisiens'] from Baudelaire's *Les Fleurs du mal*.[22] He described the typical social characters of the period in what he called 'dialectical images'. These dialectical images, these social types, were interpreted as the allegories of modernity – that is, historically created, but cut off from human intentionality – which have acquired a life of their own. This, of course, is an obvious parallel with his earlier work on Baroque allegory.

Benjamin also claimed – and this is one of the things that has become very contentious about his work – that modern allegory in a commodity-producing society is also a symptom of the fall of man. As may occur to many of you, it's not usual for a Marxist, or somebody influenced by Marxism, to believe in the inherent sinfulness of man, because Marxism, and Marx especially, had no concept of a fixed human nature. In fact, the idea of a fixed human nature was precisely one of the ideas that Marx wanted to destroy, and so have most later Marxists.[23] But one of

---

21   In *The Melancholy Science*, Rose expands on the phantasmagoric fetish-character of commodities, and how this has been lost in the English translation: 'The German translated as "the fantastic form" is *die phantasmagorische form* which should be translated as "the phantasmagoric form" in English. The epithet "phantasmagoric" stresses the personifications as well as the strangeness of the form in which the relations between men appear. "Phantasmagoria" means a crowd or succession of dim or doubtfully real persons. The word was coined in England in 1802 and was taken over later into German.' Gillian Rose, *The Melancholy Science: An Introduction to the Thought of Theodor W. Adorno* (London: Verso, 2014), p. 40.

22   *Les Fleurs du mal* (*The Flowers of Evil* in English), by the French poet Charles Baudelaire (1821–67), was written and revised between 1840 and Baudelaire's death in 1867. First published in 1857, it was condemned as offensive to public morality, and censored. The ban on six particular poems was not lifted in France until 1949. The section 'Tableaux Parisiens' contains eighteen poems, and was added to the second edition in 1861. Charles Baudelaire, *The Flowers of Evil*, transl. James N. McGowan (Oxford: Oxford University Press, 1998).

23   See, for instance, the sixth of Marx's 'Theses on Feuerbach': 'The essence of man is no abstraction inherent in each single individual. In its reality is the ensemble of the social relations.' *MECW*, vol. 5, p. 7.

the greatnesses of Benjamin's thought is his fusing, on the one hand, of
the classical religious notion of inherent sin which characterises the
human historical world, as opposed to the justified or eternal one,
together with an emphasis on the proletariat, not as the subject–object
of history, in a Lukácsian sense, but as a stage of post-history, just as the
technical reproducibility of artworks brings us to the threshold of
post-art.

Now I'm going to say a bit more about how Benjamin managed to
fuse these two points of view. In fact, he did this in the theses he
wrote just before he killed himself: the 'Theses on the Philosophy of
History.' There are eighteen of them. What he meant by inherent
human sin, or history as man's fall from grace, was really a criticism
of the Marxism of social democracy. Like Bloch, Benjamin also
thought that the defects in Marxist theory of the pre-war period had
contributed to the defeat of the working class. In these 'Theses on the
Philosophy of History', he launched a massive attack against any
evolutionary interpretation of the development of the proletariat. He
refused any belief in the inevitable triumph of the working class. He
emphasised throughout these theses the power of the class enemy.
That enemy, he said, has never ceased to be victorious [VI], and, of
course, its latest victor was fascism.[24] The past, he said, on the one
hand, must be considered as the history of the victory of these rulers;
and, on the other hand, must be seen as the cultural treasures which
these rulers and their victory have made possible [VII]. Culture, for
him, was deeply ambiguous. He said: 'There has never been a document of civilisation which is not at the same time a document of
barbarism' [VII]. He believed that it was the facile ideas of the social
democrats that the working class would inevitably win without much
activity on its own part that had contributed to its defeat. Instead, in
a way that's rather reminiscent of Bloch, Benjamin believed that it
would be necessary to blast open the continuum of history [XIV–
XVI] if there was to be a successful proletarian revolution. He understood all past revolutions – the French Revolution, for example – as

---

24   The numerals in square brackets are provided by the editors and refer to the
relevant thesis in each case.

having done that. He emphasised, like Bloch, the uniqueness of the present, and that to change it would involve a qualitative leap – a leap, he said, in the open air of history [XIV] – which would create a unique relationship to the past but could not be seen as a fulfilment of a continuous development.

That's an outline of some of Benjamin's major ideas. In some of the time left to us, I want to ask this question (which is coming at the end of the lecture, rather than the beginning): Who was Walter Benjamin? I've told you that he committed suicide in 1940. Up to that period, in 1940, Benjamin had many friends – including all the people I'm talking about in this lecture series – but he had no connections. Once his doctoral thesis had been refused, he became a freelance writer. He never had an academic job, and he was often very poor. From 1935 to 1940, after the Nazi seizure of power, Benjamin lived in Paris. During that period, he was a member of the Institute for Social Research. That's the only sense in which he can be called a member of the Frankfurt School. During that period, it was the Institute for Social Research which kept him alive, which gave him money. They tried throughout that period to get him to leave Europe, but he wouldn't, until the very last minute, after the Nazis had put him in a concentration camp for several weeks, when he was finally persuaded to flee.[25] He fled to the South of France, and he killed himself on the Spanish border.

The battle over Benjamin has already gone into three generations. The first generation consisted of these friends of his at the time, and can be divided into four schools. There's the Brecht school, who take up the aspect of Benjamin's thought which is interested in anti-illusionist art, and his politics of the proletariat as they come up in the 'Theses on the Philosophy of History'. The second school is the Frankfurt School, the Institute for Social Research, and they produced a Hegelian and Marxist interpretation and criticism of the Brecht interpretation of Benjamin. The third school is the Hannah Arendt school. Hannah Arendt was a friend of Benjamin's in Paris, and it was

---

25   As Martin Jay notes in his afterword, Benjamin was not put in a Nazi concentration camp, but a French work camp established for German citizens.

she who was responsible for the first volume of Benjamin's writings which appeared in English – the *Illuminations* volume, which you may know. She is responsible for the attempt to give a Heideggerian interpretation of Benjamin. I'll say more about that in a minute. The fourth school is the school of Gershom Scholem. I don't know if you've heard of Gershom Scholem. I'll say a bit about him in a minute. He is responsible for putting an emphasis on the Jewish and religious aspects of Benjamin's thought. These disputes have been going on since 1940, and they are continuing today.

In the English-speaking world, on the other hand, there has been the most incredible trivialisation of Benjamin. Most of the things which have been published on Benjamin in English stress the personal aspects of his life, the fact that he was incomprehensible, and, if they do talk about his ideas, they tend to stress the messianic aspects. What you can see from my discussion of Benjamin in the first half is that this is really not a way to deal with Benjamin's ideas. I'll say a bit more about that at the end.

On Benjamin and the Brecht school: Benjamin was an ardent enthusiast of Brecht's notion of epic theatre. He wrote several articles trying to clarify and develop Brecht's notion of anti-illusionist art, and I'm going to discuss this more in my lecture on Brecht.[26] Benjamin was interested in Brecht's attempts to purify and simplify language; Brecht's use of the new technological media to ridicule the old artistic forms, and to create wholly new forms. He was interested in Brecht's idea of developing a functional art – an art which would serve a specific purpose, and which would be directly integrated or reintegrated into social contexts of use. He was interested in the attempt to liberate the masses from the power and authority of traditional art. But Brecht himself was not entirely comfortable with Benjamin's theoretical underpinning of his work. In fact, he refused to publish Benjamin's article, 'The Work of Art in the Age of Mechanical Reproduction', in the journal which he edited.[27]

---

26   See Benjamin, *Understanding Brecht.*

27   As Martin Jay notes in his afterword, this is not strictly true. It was in fact another of *Das Wort*'s editors, Willi Bredel, who rejected Benjamin's 'Work of Art' essay.

Benjamin was also a very close friend of Adorno's, and the rest of the Frankfurt School. As I've said, it was the Frankfurt School who financed Benjamin in the second half of the 1930s. They published about five of his articles in the Institute's journal, the *Journal for Social Research*. Adorno and Benjamin also corresponded throughout the '30s over Benjamin's work on Paris. In this correspondence, that has now been published, Adorno made several very striking criticisms of Benjamin's approach – of Benjamin's understanding of Lukács and commodity fetishism.[28] He thought Benjamin's work, especially the emphasis on dialectical images, was too descriptive, and not theoretical enough; that Benjamin's interpretation of reification as phantasmagoria and as producing the dialectical images of social types produced a static and archaic analysis of society – or rather, it didn't produce any analysis at all, but rested on static and archaic presuppositions. He thought that Benjamin's making of reification into a vision of social characters reduced reification to a fact of people's consciousness, and it obscured the determining structural factors of the mode of production. Finally, he thought that Benjamin's idea that the new technological means of reproducing art would totally transform art and people's perception of it was hopelessly naive. He thought it was far more likely that, instead of mechanical reproduction producing a new form of liberation of art, it would produce new forms of domination. Adorno was also opposed to Brecht's influence on Benjamin for the same reasons. Adorno was accused, both during Benjamin's lifetime and afterwards, in his editing and commentary on Benjamin's work, of playing down the Brechtian and proletarian aspects, and thereby distorting his thought.[29]

---

28   See Theodor W. Adorno and Walter Benjamin, *The Complete Correspondence: 1928–1940*, ed. Henri Lonitz, transl. Nicholas Walker (Cambridge, MA: Harvard University Press, 2001). For a more focused selection of this correspondence, and an enlightening editorial introduction, see 'Presentation III' (transl. Harry Zohn) in Theodor Adorno, Walter Benjamin, Ernst Bloch, Bertolt Brecht, and Georg Lukács, *Aesthetics and Politics* (London: Verso, 1980), pp. 100–41.

29   See, in particular, Helmut Heissenbüttel, 'Vom Zeugnis des Fortlebens in Briefen', *Merkur* 21: 228 (March 1967), pp. 232–44. The German novelist Heissenbüttel (1921–1996) charges Adorno's editorship with erasing the Brechtian materialism and Marxism from Benjamin's writings.

Now I'd like to say something very briefly about Benjamin and Scholem, and Benjamin and Hannah Arendt.

Scholem is the only person so far who has written a biography of Benjamin.[30] Scholem himself was Benjamin's friend before the First World War, but he has subsequently become known for creating the study of Jewish mysticism as a scholarly and academic discipline. He is, at present, professor of Jewish Mysticism at the Hebrew University in Jerusalem.[31] During Benjamin's lifetime and afterwards, he has always stressed the kabbalistic, messianic, Jewish aspects of Benjamin's thought. He was opposed to Brecht's influence on Benjamin, and he was also opposed to the Frankfurt School's influence on Benjamin.

Hannah Arendt, as I've mentioned, wrote the famous introduction to *Illuminations*, and the second volume of selections from Benjamin's essays which has just been published – *Reflections* – was also chosen by Hannah Arendt just before she died. She is responsible for the infuriating stress on the personal aspects of Benjamin's life, and also for a Heideggerian interpretation of Benjamin – that is, an aspect which plays down the political and Marxist aspects of his thought and stresses his views on language and truth. She was opposed to the Brecht interpretation, the Frankfurt School interpretation, and the Scholem interpretation.[32]

A picture has emerged of a tortured Benjamin, torn between his friends, who, in their turn, resented each other's influence, who did not appreciate Benjamin's originality, and who eventually drove him

---

30   Gershom Scholem, *Walter Benjamin: The Story of a Friendship*, transl. Harry Zohn (New York: NYRB, 2001). More biographies have followed, such as Momme Brodersen, *Walter Benjamin: A Biography*, transl. Malcolm R. Green and Ingrida Ligers (London: Verso, 1996); Leslie, *Walter Benjamin*; Howard Eiland and Michael W. Jennings, *Walter Benjamin: A Critical Life* (Cambridge, MA: Harvard University Press, 2016). See also Gershom Scholem, ed., *The Correspondence of Walter Benjamin and Gershom Scholem: 1932–1940*, transl. Gary Smith and Andre Lefevere (Cambridge, MA: Harvard University Press, 1992).

31   Scholem died in 1982, aged eighty-four.

32   See the acrimonious correspondence between Arendt and Adorno on the legacy of Benjamin, and on who had the right to edit his work. 'On Walter Benjamin's Legacy: A Correspondence between Hannah Arendt and Theodor Adorno', ed. Susan H. Gillespie and Samantha Rose Hill, *Los Angeles Review of Books*, 9 December 2019.

to suicide. It is often said that Benjamin was schizophrenic, in relation to his interest in Marxism, and to his interest in religion.[33] This
is a totally false picture. Benjamin was not a victim of his friends'
interest in him. He enjoyed the diversity of his friends and his arguments with them. He had, in fact, tried to kill himself many times
before he eventually succeeded.

What is Benjamin's importance? It is certainly not the split between
Marxism and Judaism or messianism in his thought. Far more interesting in Benjamin's work are the contradictions and clashes between
the different kinds of modernism which he espoused. I said at the
beginning of the lecture that he was both interested in the modernism of parody and pastiche, intensely involved with a rearrangement
of the old forms; and, on the other extreme, he was interested in a
modernism of technological innovation – the notion of a post-
aesthetic art which would rest on wholly changed forms, which would
have a wholly different function in society. But there were contradictions in his espousal of these different forms of modernism. For
example, in the famous introduction to the *Trauerspiel* book, which
we discussed earlier, Benjamin argues against an instrumental view
of method and art; but in his Brechtian period and writings, he argues
for a new functional art. In his 'Theses on the Philosophy of History',
Benjamin argues against those kinds of Marxism which underesti-
mate the power of the enemy in their theory of the inevitable victory
of the working class; but in his writings on technological reproduction – I don't know if anybody's noticed this as I've been talking – he
assumes that a changed art could prevail and revolutionise people's
perceptions regardless of the power of other social institutions. He
overestimates the power of a changed art to change the rest of society.
He concentrates on the masses, and forgets that the masses are not yet

---

33   Many commentators have claimed that the tension between Benjamin's
Marxism and his Judaism or messianism was unresolved. See, for instance, Rolf
Tiedemann, 'Historical Materialism or Political Messianism? An Interpretation of
the Theses "On the Concept of History" ', *Philosophical Forum* 15: 1–2 (1983), pp.
71–104, and Jürgen Habermas, 'Walter Benjamin: Consciousness-Raising or
Rescuing Critique', in Gary Smith, ed., *On Walter Benjamin: Critical Essays and
Recollections* (Cambridge, MA: MIT, 1991), pp. 90–128.

victorious. I think this comes from his application of an analysis of technology in a communist society, from transferring a *Proletkult* argument from Russia to Germany.

In the last two weeks, we have examined Lukács and his blanket rejection of modernism in art and in theory. We've also looked at Bloch's uncritical acceptance of the cause of expressionism in art and theory. Benjamin helps us to see that the modernist position, like the classic one, has its own fundamental contradictions. It was Adorno and Horkheimer, a generation younger than Lukács, Bloch, and Brecht, who provided the sociological and Marxist analysis of the contradictions of the Marxist modernist position in its relation to advanced capitalist society. In the next lecture, which will not be next week but on March 1, I will be discussing the book by Horkheimer and Adorno, *Dialectic of Enlightenment*.

5

The Dialectic of Enlightenment: Horkheimer and Adorno

Editorial note

The recording starts shortly after the start of this lecture, but the missing content can be reconstructed with reference to what Rose goes on to argue, and her earlier work on Adorno in The Melancholy Science *(1978).*

Rose begins the lecture by anticipating four common misconceptions regarding Adorno and Horkheimer's 1947 work, Dialectic of Enlightenment. *The fourth misconception is included in the recording (and therefore the transcript, below). We know that the third misconception concerns 'the connection between* The Authoritarian Personality *and this chapter on anti-Semitism' – that is, the connection between Adorno's 1950 sociological study of the personality traits endemic to fascism, and the fifth chapter of* Dialectic of Enlightenment. *Rose goes on in the lecture to say that Adorno's* The Authoritarian Personality *was criticised at the time as a work of empirical sociology, for spuriously presupposing the idea of an 'authoritarian personality' without explaining it at a 'macro-level' and thus reducing it to a 'psychological syndrome.' She explains, however, that this misconception is cleared up by the work in the chapter on anti-Semitism in* Dialectic of Enlightenment. *This is developed in more detail below.*

The two other misconceptions are likely to concern Adorno's attitudes towards music, on the one hand, and the importance of Nietzsche to the Dialectic of Enlightenment's *argument, on the other. Firstly, throughout these lectures, Rose rejects the misconception that Adorno hated jazz and popular music while heralding the revolutionary potential of the avant-garde. Rose demonstrates that, in fact, Adorno was critical of both popular and avant-garde music. Secondly, Rose demonstrates in* The Melancholy Science *that 'the notion of a "dialectic of enlightenment" is an interpretation of Nietzsche, and not of Max Weber, and the emphasis on the social imposition of concepts is also based on an interpretation of Nietzsche not of Durkheim.'[1] This links to Rose's point in the introductory lecture on the importance of Nietzsche to Adorno and Horkheimer, and critical theory more generally:*

> *Nietzsche rejected a philosophy of history based on the Hegelian idea of an ultimate telos or goal in history, of an ideal society in the future, or of the reconciliation of all contradictions. Nietzsche rejected that position. He applied the notion of contradiction to the optimistic philosophy of history itself – for example, that the process of historical change might turn into the opposite of all the ideals. This is what Horkheimer and Adorno were later to call 'the dialectic of Enlightenment.'[2]*

... so, in a sense, they were asking for problems, and they certainly got them. We're going to discuss that – the connection between *The Authoritarian Personality* and this chapter on anti-Semitism.

The fourth misunderstanding which has been associated with this book is this funny notion of the 'culture industry'.[3] In fact, there's an article in English – I hope it's on your reading list – in which Adorno

---

1   Gillian Rose, *The Melancholy Science: An Introduction to the Thought of Theodor W. Adorno* (London: Verso, 2014), p. 34.

2   Pp. 17–18 of this volume.

3   See Theodor Adorno and Max Horkheimer, 'The Culture Industry: Enlightenment as Mass Deception', in *Dialectic of Enlightenment: Philosophical Fragments*, transl. Edmund Jephcott, ed. Gunzelin Schmid Noerr (Stanford, CA: Stanford University Press, 2002), pp. 94–136.

took the very phrase back because it had caused so many misconceptions. (Yes, under 'Adorno' there's a heading called 'The Culture Industry Reconsidered' – that's an article which has been translated in *New German Critique* – and in that article, which was written about twenty years later, Adorno says that it had caused so many misconceptions – this notion of the culture industry – that he took it back.)[4] Nevertheless, it has become quite a famous phrase. It's a rather odd phrase in English, isn't it? We'd be more likely to say, the 'entertainment industry', or something like that. As with Adorno's work on anti-Semitism, what actually goes in this chapter on the culture industry, if you read it in isolation, from the rest of Adorno's works on aesthetics, it looks like an extremely harsh criticism of jazz, popular culture, pop music, and so on. In fact, it's Adorno's major criticism of Benjamin – Benjamin's notion of what changes the new mechanical modes of reproduction of artworks would make – which is developed in this chapter. Adorno applied his criticism not just to popular culture, but to so-called avant-garde art or modernist art – the expressionism we've been discussing in other lectures. Unfortunately, it's very easy to misread what Adorno says on the culture industry if you don't know about the rest of his aesthetics.

All in all, this sounds like a terrible tale, doesn't it? All four issues in this book have given rise to very serious misunderstandings. I'm going to try and develop a discussion of this book in the other contexts in which we've been looking at these issues, so that when you do pick it up – I hope you will have a go at it, because it's a most incredible book – you will see some of the ways *not* to read it.

In this book, Horkheimer and Adorno were writing ten years later than all the people we've been considering so far. They wrote this book in the '40s. The things we've been discussing so far – the Lukács, the Bloch, and the Benjamin – have all been things written in the '30s. In

---

4   Theodor W. Adorno, 'The Culture Industry Reconsidered', transl. Anson G. Rabinbach, *New German Critique* 6 (Autumn 1975), pp. 12–19. The idea that Adorno 'took back' the term 'culture industry' is perhaps misleading. In 'The Culture Industry Reconsidered', he does not retract the term, but rather qualifies it, and justifies why he did not refer instead to 'mass culture'.

it, they criticise the positions of Lukács, Bloch, and Benjamin, on their philosophy of history, their theory of late-capitalist society, and their aesthetics. Now, just to recapitulate what we had established in these respects: Lukács saw the period of fascism's success as a period of disintegration and decadence; Bloch, on the other hand, saw it as a period of disintegration, but stressed its nature as a period of transition; and Benjamin, as a third alternative, on the one hand, considered that new forms of technology of the period would have a liberating potential, but, on the other hand, he stressed that the class enemy had not ceased to be victorious. Horkheimer and Adorno, generalising not only from the experience of fascism in Germany, but also from their experience of exile in America, stressed this period – that is, the '30s and the '40s – as one in which new forms of domination were being consolidated; a period of increasing stability, not disintegration. They considered that the new technology would be used for regressive and not for progressive ends. Far from providing an ahistorical account, they were in fact trying to isolate those institutions which they foresaw would persist after the defeat of fascism. However, in this book, especially in Chapters 2 and 3, they did use examples from other epochs – they went back even to classical Greece – to illustrate specific syndromes.[5] This is quite a standard method in social analysis, that in order to bring out a syndrome which you think has become dominant in contemporary society, you might in fact discuss a simpler society or a primitive society where the syndrome can be analysed more clearly. The fact that Adorno developed this notion of dialectic of enlightenment in relationship to Homer should not prevent us from seeing that it essentially applies to his theory of late-capitalist society.

What does this funny title, *Dialectic of Enlightenment*, mean? By 'enlightenment', first of all, Horkheimer and Adorno are not trying to refer to any strict sort of eighteenth-century sense. There's only one or two references to Voltaire in this book. But I think they were thinking of a very famous article by Kant – it's very short, you could even

---

5   These chapters are entitled 'Excursus I: Odysseus or Myth and Enlightenment' (pp. 35–62) and 'Excursus II: Juliette or Enlightenment and Morality' (pp. 63–93).

look at it – called 'What Is Enlightenment?'[6] This article by Kant – although I'm not claiming that I'm explaining it – puts forward four features which are associated with the kind of rationalism which Kant and other writers were hoping for:

- a notion of rationalism which rejects the authority of tradition or myth – it tended to be anti-clerical;
- a notion of rationalism which stressed the autonomy of the individual and his right to make his own decisions;
- a notion of rationalism which promised increasing control over the natural world, with an emphasis on natural science;
- a notion of rationalism which promised an increasingly just organisation of society.

These were the original promises which the concept of rationalism, on which enlightenment depends, had seemed to hold out. Incorporated in this notion of enlightenment is a reference to Max Weber's sociology of rationality, especially Weber's notion of the disenchantment of the world. By this, Weber meant that in a modern capitalist society, legal, rational institutions would be the paradigmatic institutions of authority, replacing the traditional authority of pre-capitalist society. [Under] 'enlightenment', Horkheimer and Adorno also included this reference to Weber's sociology of legal, rational institutions.[7]

That's the ideal of enlightenment, but what did Horkheimer and Adorno mean by the '*dialectic* of enlightenment'? What they meant by it is not what dialectic means generally. As you know, 'dialectic' is a very slippery word, and I'm not going to try to say what it means. But what 'dialectic' means in this phrase – 'dialectic of enlightenment'

---

6   In 1783, the *Berlinische Monatsschrift* (Berlin monthly) issued a content call for articles on the topic 'Was ist Aufklärung?' (What is enlightenment?). Kant's response to the question was published a year later. Immanuel Kant, 'An Answer to the Question: What Is Enlightenment?', in *Practical Philosophy*, transl. Mary J. Gregor (Cambridge: Cambridge University Press, 1999), pp. 11–22.

7   See especially Max Weber, *Economy and Society: An Outline of Interpretive Sociology*, transl. Keith Tribe (Cambridge, MA: Harvard University Press, 2019).

– is the following: that instead of these ideals of enlightenment bringing liberation, these social forms have become a new species of domination, new forms of enslavement, and therefore – of course, they're
playing with words – new forms of myth. I'm going to repeat that.
Instead of bringing the new kind of liberation which these ideals
originally seemed to promise, they turned into new forms of social
control and domination – new modes of enslavement; and, because
of this, because they'd turned into the opposite of what they promised, Horkheimer and Adorno said that the original ideas had become
a new kind of myth – whereas, as I said, enlightenment was meant to
be a notion which was opposed to myth.

The rationalism of control over nature had instead become means
of political control over men, such as weapons of destruction. Instead
of a just organisation of society based on formal abstract notions of
equality, the organisation of society based on enlightenment had
turned into new ways of perpetuating real inequality. Instead of the
autonomy of mind which had been promised, new ways of control-
ling the minds of others had been developed, new forms of propaganda and lies. Instead of the growth of legal, rational institutions,
there had been the growth of forms of control which are in fact unintelligible to those that submit to them. Enlightenment has turned into
its opposite. As I say, while Horkheimer and Adorno traced this back
to the eighteenth century, and even to Homer, they were plainly
concerned with the same period as Bloch and Lukács, which they
were able to extend by ten years, and it's significant that they did so
from America, and not from Europe.

What are the consequences of this position for political analysis? I'm
now going to say something which is slightly scandalous. This view of
Horkheimer's and Adorno's is in opposition to what has become a very
standard but, I think, extremely facile liberal, functional explanation of
fascism. I'm going to give you an example of the sort of book where this
explanation is given. It's a book by Ralf Dahrendorf called *Society and
Democracy in Germany*, published in 1965.[8] Dahrendorf, in this book,

---

8   Ralf Dahrendorf, *Society and Democracy in Germany* (London: W. W. Norton,
1979).

gives an explanation of the reason why fascism occurred in Germany, which is quite a normal explanation. This normal explanation says that, in Germany (as opposed to, say, Britain or France or other countries) there was a divorce between the late and extremely rapid development of capitalism – you presumably know that the industrial revolution in Germany only really occurred at the end of the nineteenth century – and the archaic feudal political institutions which Germany had, i.e. there was a lack of liberal tradition in Germany. You had a very rapid development of capitalism without a liberal-democratic political struc-ture. That's a very standard explanation of this accelerated industrial development leading to the breakdown of civilisation in fascism. Fascism became a mode of modernisation in Germany.

The Frankfurt School position, with this notion of the dialectic of enlightenment, is a massive challenge to that position in the follow-ing sense: that is, the Frankfurt School – by this I mean, of course, Horkheimer and Adorno – are implying that it is capitalist rationality itself which produces and reproduces forms of barbarism; that fascism cannot be seen as a breakdown unique to Germany due to the asymmetry in Germany's social institutions, but is itself inherent in the logic of late capitalism. That's one of the reasons why this title, *Dialectic of Enlightenment*, was so polemical and contentious. That's really what this notion of dialectic of enlightenment is claiming: that precisely those aspects of eighteenth-century culture which we were most proud of are those which have turned into the kind of social institutions which could produce fascism. Fascism can't be seen as a breakdown in them, but as part of their logic.

However, as you can see, this theory of the dialectic of enlighten-ment is not based on a class analysis. Instead, Horkheimer and Adorno – and in this sense they are very much like Lukács, Bloch, and Benjamin – set out to analyse the development of those forms of domination which they believed had prevented the formation of class consciousness. Their use of concepts of mass society must be seen in that light. The concept of mass society has so many reac-tionary overtones, so it's important to see that in this book the emphasis is always on why the classic proletarian class conscious-ness has not developed.

In particular, their analysis of these forms of domination occurs in this chapter called 'The Culture Industry' – 'Enlightenment as Mass Deception' is the subtitle. The very title of this chapter, 'Enlightenment as Mass Deception' – if you remember from the last lecture – is a rude riposte to Benjamin's idea that the age of mechanical reproduction would promise a new form of liberation or enlightenment. If you think of it in connection with Benjamin, you can see that it's not just eighteenth-century notions of enlightenment that Adorno and Horkheimer were criticising, but the views of people like Benjamin and Brecht that new forms of mechanical reproduction would lead to a new enlightenment in the twentieth century. Similarly, in this chapter, 'Elements of Anti-Semitism,' it's also developed in opposition to Lukács, Benjamin, and Bloch.[9] This is partly done by analysing fascism in countries other than Germany. You may imagine how bold it was in the '40s, when the war was still continuing, to say that you could analyse fascist potential in America. That was another reason why the work of Adorno and Horkheimer created such a stir. As in the case of the other writers we have been discussing, the question of the possibility of cultural experience is, for Horkheimer and Adorno, inseparable from their analysis of fascism.

Since, as I said at the beginning of this lecture, these two chapters here, Chapter 4 and Chapter 5, have been so misunderstood because they're only half of an analysis, which depends on work they were doing elsewhere, I'm going to discuss these two chapters in connection with other sources.[10] I'm not just going to rely on *Dialectic of Enlightenment*, I'm going to try and show how the central ideas in *Dialectic of Enlightenment* sit with the other works which they were doing at the same time. If anybody afterwards wants to know what the other sources are, you're very welcome to come and ask me.

The theory of anti-Semitism, which I'm going to discuss first, is inseparable from the work that Adorno was doing on *The*

---

9   Theodor Adorno and Max Horkheimer, 'Elements of Anti-Semitism: Limits of Enlightenment', in *Dialectic of Enlightenment*, pp. 137–72.

10   The two chapters being 'The Culture Industry' and 'Elements of Anti-Semitism: Limits of Enlightenment'.

Authoritarian Personality, in which, as I've mentioned, he and three others had the audacity to analyse fascist potential in America in the 1940s. This book, *The Authoritarian Personality* – which I haven't put on the reading list, but is still in print and widely available – is quite well known as a piece of empirical sociology which claims to measure the antidemocratic potential of the individual, the American individual in this case, locating a specified disposition by utilising a range of related interview scales. The major criticisms of the book were that the notion of fascist or authoritarian personality is presupposed but not demonstrated by the empirical tests, and that it fails to explain authoritarianism at the macro level, relying instead on depicting a psychological syndrome. Adorno responded to these criticisms of *The Authoritarian Personality* by referring to this chapter in *Dialectic of Enlightenment*, 'Elements of Anti-Semitism', which he said developed the theoretical background.

This chapter in *Dialectic of Enlightenment* circles around the proposition that 'bourgeois anti-Semitism has a specific economic reason: the concealment of domination in production'.[11] I'm going to try and explain what he meant by that. (It's both of them.[12] If I say one I mean them both.) The capitalist is judged by the worker to engage in productive labour, but, as Marx argued, profit, the return to capital, is not correctly regarded as a return to productive labour. Marx considered that only the worker is a productive labourer – that is, actually producing new values in a society. The Jews were, for a long time, excluded from owning the means of production, but they were allowed to own much of the circulation sector. This role as middleman, as intermediary, is more visible to the worker in the sphere of commerce and consumption than the role of the capitalist, but less intelligible to him as an essential function of capitalism, for it is easier for the worker to understand the immediate function of the production of goods, but less easy to understand the intermediary function of commerce: advertising, financial techniques, etc. It is easier to understand the relationship between wages and prices – that is, what you can buy with

---

11   Adorno and Horkheimer, *Dialectic of Enlightenment*, p. 142.
12   That is, both Adorno and Horkheimer.

your wages – than to understand the relationship between the worker's own productive labour and the wages received for it. Hence,
Horkheimer and Adorno argued, economic injustice of the whole
capitalist class is attributed to the Jews. They are regarded by the
masses as non-productive parasites: 'The merchant [that is, the Jew]
presents them [the workers] with the bill which they have signed away
to the manufacturer. The merchant becomes the bailiff of the whole
system and takes the hatred of others upon himself. The responsibility
of the circulation sector is a socially necessary illusion [or ideology].'[13]

In late-capitalist society, the growth of large organisations dimin-
ishes the role of the intermediary, the sphere of circulation, since
production and distribution come to be dominated and controlled by
strong centralised agencies. Hence, there was no longer any economic
need for the Jews, but there was certainly a need to attribute to them
the crises of the whole system, such as those of the interwar period,
by reviving the image of the non-productive parasite.

If you read this chapter in *Dialectic of Enlightenment*, you'll wonder
where the hell I got all this from. What I've tried to do is bring out as
rigorously as possible the theory that is underlying it.

The rest of this chapter in *Dialectic of Enlightenment* develops a
psychoanalytic theory of anti-Semitism as a projection of the change
in the mode of domination onto the Jews, as a projection of new
forms of impotence, as Marx revealed religion itself to be a projection
of social impotence. Projection is not only a projection in Marx's
sense of what is denied – power – but also a projection of what is
desired and feared. Projection is not only, as in Marx's sense, a projection which controls the exploited, but it also expresses the needs and
fears of the exploiters. The theory of projection is predicated on a
general theory of the individual's loss of autonomy. Fascism is understood as an extreme case of such a loss of autonomy, which Adorno
explicated by means of the model of 'narcissistic identification'.[14]

---

13   Adorno and Horkheimer, *Dialectic of Enlightenment*, pp. 142–3. Translation
altered. Interjections in square brackets are Rose's own.

14   In Freudian psychoanalysis, identification is a process whereby someone
assimilates an attribute of another and is transformed by it. As suggested here,

Fascist propaganda mobilised 'unconscious, regressive processes' in a specific way which did not represent 'the return of the archaic, but its reproduction in and by civilisation itself' in a planned and calculated way.[15]

What I've tried to do in explicating this theory of anti-Semitism is to argue against the charge that Horkheimer and Adorno merely reduced it to a psychological explanation, and to show that they did try to give a structural explanation of anti-Semitism; that only secondarily, having analysed the economic basis for anti-Semitism, did they go on to use psychoanalytic concepts.

Now, in the time that's left, I want to talk about this concept of the 'culture industry'. As I say, this concept has been widely misunderstood because it is only one-half of Adorno's aesthetic theory. It has been read as an attack on popular culture, jazz, and popular music. Adorno's view differed from Benjamin, Lukács, and Bloch, in that, unlike them, he was neither wholly in favour of modernism or expressionism in art, like Bloch and Benjamin, but nor was he wholly opposed to it. He produced an extremely powerful sociology which examined precisely the contradictions within modernist or expressionist works. In the lecture which I'm going to give on Adorno, I will go into that side of his aesthetics much more. Today, I'm going to try and explain what he meant by the culture industry. It links up very much with our discussion of Walter Benjamin. You may remember that Benjamin was very interested in the ways in which, in an age of the mechanical reproduction of artworks, 'to an even greater degree the work of art reproduced becomes the work of art

---

narcissistic identification refers specifically to the identification which occurs following a loss of someone or something. In Freud's words, loss 'establish[es] an *identification* of the ego with the abandoned object'. Sigmund Freud, 'Mourning and Melancholia', in *The Standard Edition of the Complete Psychological Works of Sigmund Freud*, vol. 14, *On the History of the Psycho-Analytic Movement, Papers on Metapsychology and Other Works (1914–1916)*, ed. and transl. James Strachey (London: Hogarth, 2001), p. 249.

15   Adorno quoted in Rose, *Melancholy Science*, p. 135.

designed for reproducibility'.[16] You may remember that Benjamin thought that the new modes of production and reception of works of art could and would coincide for revolutionary ends. Adorno, on the other hand, interpreted the changes wrought by the mechanical reproducibility of art in quite different terms. Reproduction was not significant to him as a mechanical or technological change. He interpreted it quite differently. He considered that it would result in new modes of distribution, and in new modes of consumption or reception of works – that is, in new forms of social behaviour. This is what he called the culture industry. For Adorno, new modes of mechanical repro-duction did not mean a new kind of liberating possibility in art, but he predicted, or, rather, he analysed, the ways in which it resulted in new forms of distribution and reception – something, you may remember, that Benjamin rather naively didn't go into. This is what he called the culture industry.

He believed that these new developments constituted new forms of social and political control, and not new possibilities for emanci-pation. He insisted above all that avant-garde art and popular art, so-called, in both cases, should be examined in relationship to each other, because – and this is a really important quotation – 'both are torn halves of an integral freedom to which, however, they do not add up'.[17] This split of art into the so-called avant-garde, on the one hand, and so-called popular art, on the other, are 'torn halves of an integral freedom to which, however, they do not add up'. I'm going to keep coming back to explicating that rather striking proposition. Adorno thought you'll never understand expressionist or avant-garde art unless you understand popular art, and vice versa. But, unfortunately, in *Dialectic of Enlightenment*, he doesn't follow his own rule, and all he does is look at the popular side of it, which is why this book has

---

16   Walter Benjamin, 'The Work of Art in the Age of Mechanical Reproduction', in *Illuminations*, ed. Hannah Arendt, transl. Harry Zohn (New York: Schocken, 2007), p. 224.

17   Adorno's letter to Benjamin, 18 March 1936, in Theodor W. Adorno and Walter Benjamin, *The Complete Correspondence: 1928–1940*, ed. Henri Lonitz, transl. Nicholas Walker (Cambridge, MA: Harvard University Press, 2001) p. 130.

been read as an attack on popular art. In fact, Adorno was equally critical of so-called avant-garde art. By the end of this lecture series, I hope you'll have a picture of what he said about both sides of it. In *Dialectic of Enlightenment*, Adorno only looks at one of these torn halves, and that is so-called popular culture, or the culture industry, which he believed had been created by the new modes of mechanical reproduction of artworks.

Adorno used the classic Marxist distinctions: forces of production, and relations of production. As a force of production, mechanical reproduction may be considered in terms of the technology which produces the radio, the cinema, and the gramophone; but as a relation of production (and this is what he thought Benjamin didn't consider it as; that Benjamin only considered the new modes of mechanical reproduction as forces of production, not as relations of production) they must be considered as new modes of distribution, which presuppose the dominant mode of production and exchange in society. Thus, mechanical reproduction also permits the reproduction and larger distribution and exchange of works of art which formerly were not reproducible according to the prevailing norms of exchange, thereby increasing their commodity character. Far from, as Benjamin said, new modes of mechanical reproduction reducing the commodity character of works, Adorno thought that works would be even more sucked into commodity relations in a capitalist society.

A change in the realm of production of works of art also depends on the prevalent conditions of exchange, hence on the dominant mode of production of all other commodities in society. Adorno does not say what that is in terms of the social relations of work, manufacturing, or the buying and selling of labour power. He divides production of works of art into two types. These are the two 'torn halves'. On the one hand, composition: the development of new techniques designed to avoid the new technology, not to make use of it, and designed to avoid the prevailing norms of exchange, distribution, and consumption (that would be avant-garde art); and [on the other hand] the culture industry (that is, the producing of works for reproduction and mass consumption). Composition, in this sense, is a force of production as much as mechanical reproduction. The culture industry, in this sense, is oriented to the prevalent relations of production – that is, to the widespread norms of reception and consumption of art in society. This perspective is quite odd in several ways – that is, odd in relation to the classic Marxist use of the distinction between forces of production and relations of production. Art is counted partly as production when, in standard Marxist terms, it would be counted as part of the superstructure, and hence fall under the relations of production. Innovation in artistic and musical production is judged in terms of the significance accorded to the dominant relations of production, and the designation 'force of production' is really reserved for what resists those relations, and not for new techniques or new technology as such. But 'composition' is not a relational term in the way that 'work' or 'labour-power' are for Marx. In the realm of consumption, the culture industry is a force of production, in the sense that it constitutes a changed form of social domination and control, while, considered under the relations of production, it is responsible for kinds of social behaviour which Adorno examined by using Freudian categories.

I know that's all a bit abstract, so I'm going to give you an example of how the culture industry works. I'm taking my example from music. Adorno gives quite a few examples of how the new form of distribution which he called the culture industry would affect and change the meaning of music; how the meaning of music could be altered by the new medium of reproduction, whether the music is performed in the concert hall or broadcast on the radio. This exposition – and I hope that those of you who are not musicians can follow this – depends on a contrast between the technical notion of intelligibility established by classical music and the different norm of intelligibility which tends to be demanded when music is received by the untrained ear. Adorno's argument is that, given the current mode of exchange and distribution of music, music is adjusted at the stage of reproduction in order to gain the greatest intelligibility in the second sense – that is, the untrained sense – which may amount to the least intelligibility in the first sense – that is, the trained sense. Now I'll give you an example. In classical music, especially the symphonic form of the sonata, the intelligibility of the whole composition depends on the development of a theme, which is accomplished by details which have an independent life, but which are ultimately apprehended in terms of the overall structure of the piece: 'the melodic content of the basic rhythm, that is to say, the intervals which constitute it, change perpetually'.[18] Romantic music – and this is Adorno's model for pop music, too – by contrast, detaches the detail in a piece of music by increased use of chromaticism, so that the detail itself, rather than its relation to the whole, becomes the unit of expression, which, together with exaggerated contrasts and stress on sound colour, is easier to grasp. Adorno demonstrates that all music, whether classical, romantic, or popular, tends to be adjusted in the process of reproduction to the most easily intelligible standard. Thus, separable themes, strong colour, spectacular sound, and single melodic lines are emphasised. Adorno calls this 'standardisation', 'fetishism in music' – that is, of course, a reference to Marx's view of commodity fetishism – and 'the regression of listening'.[19] The loss of unity in the music, and the shift of meaning from the totality to the individual moments, produces an atomised mode of listening (apprehension) or quotation listening, as easily memorisable elements are loosened from the whole. Works become 'conglomerates of tunes of both sensual richness and structural poverty', which render 'unnecessary the process of thinking' which was needed to comprehend the overall structure of classical music.[20] In the case of the older music, an attitude is produced in the listener 'which leads him to seek colour and stimulating sounds. Music, however, composed in structural rather than colouristic terms, does not satisfy these mechanised claims.'[21]

Popular music, by which Adorno understood jazz and other forms of what he called 'light' or entertainment music – and, you must remember, Adorno was writing in 1944, so he didn't know as much

18   Theodor W. Adorno, 'The Radio Symphony: An Experiment in Theory', in *Current of Music: Elements of a Radio Theory* (Malden: Polity, 2009), p. 151.

19   See Theodor W. Adorno, 'On the Fetish Character in Music and the Regression of Listening', in *Essays on Music*, ed. Richard Leppert (Berkeley: University of California Press, 2002), pp. 288–317.

20   Adorno, 'Radio Symphony', pp. 159–60.

21   Ibid., p. 160.

pop music as we do – is composed according to these standardised claims. Standardisation in this kind of music means that the overall theme is clearly stated at the beginning of the piece, so that the details do not develop the theme, but merely repeat it, and have no special status within the whole work, hence the emphasis on beat and repeatable rhythm.

That's a slightly more technical or detailed example of exactly what sort of effect Adorno thought the culture industry had on the reproduction of works of art. You should contrast it with Benjamin's predictions about what effects reproduction would have on the work of art. Adorno went on to suggest that the desire for these forms of easily intelligible music, or other forms of art, is determined by the mode of production and the work process. People are themselves 'products of the same mechanisms which determine the production of popular music'.[22] They treat their spare time as a means to reproduce their working activity, and 'they want standardised goods and pseudo-individualisation, because leisure is an escape from work and at the same time is moulded after those psychological attitudes to which their workaday world exclusively habituates them'.[23]

Now, Adorno never examines the work process, nor does he differentiate between different kinds of work experience – that is, between class and music. You see, what happened is that this is only one side of Adorno's sociology of art: his critique of popular entertainment music, or classical music to the extent that it is romanticised by the media. This is what comes in this book *Dialectic of Enlightenment*, but it's less than one-half of Adorno's sociology of art. As a result of this book, which people tend to know more than other books by Horkheimer and Adorno, Adorno got the reputation of being an attacker of popular art, and some kind of defender of the cause of avant-garde art or privileged art. That, in fact, is not true. In the lecture on Adorno, we will see that Adorno was just as critical of

---

22   Theodor W. Adorno, with the assistance of George Simpson, 'On Popular Music' (1941), in *Essays on Music*, p. 458.

23   Ibid., pp. 458–9.

modernism and expressionism as he was of the so-called culture industry.

Just by means of conclusion, I'd just like to summarise again why *Dialectic of Enlightenment* has become such a central and shocking book for the Frankfurt School. It is because – if you recall our discussion of the actual phrase 'dialectic of enlightenment' – it's not just the enlightenment, but also Hegel's and Marx's philosophy of history which Horkheimer and Adorno expose as having turned into the opposite of what they promised. It's not just the enlightenment that is implicated in this dialectic, but also Hegel and Marx's predictions about the possibility of progress in history.

Another reason why this book is very important – and this may connect up with something some of you have read – is that it had an immense influence on Marcuse, and especially on his book *One-Dimensional Man*.[24] If you think about the book *One-Dimensional Man* in connection with what we've been discussing today, you'll see that many of its central theses were, relatively speaking, a popularisation of these ideas which Horkheimer and Adorno developed ten years earlier.

Another reason why this book had such an enormous influence, which we haven't really gone into today, is the use of Weber's concept of rationality. Lukács, in *History and Class Consciousness*, also used Weber's critique of rationality as part of his critique of capitalist rationality, but Lukács concluded that the proletariat had an opportunity of escaping from this logic of domination, whereas Horkheimer and Adorno concluded that they had no such possibility – or rather, they took up Benjamin's view that the enemy has never ceased to be victorious, and that socialism will be extremely irresponsible if it develops facile philosophies of history which imply that social-democratic parties only have to sit back and the working class will be victorious.

The biggest reason why this book was shocking, was because it was based on the thesis that fascism represents the modernisation of barbarism, and not a relapse into it.

---

24   Herbert Marcuse, *One-Dimensional Man: Studies in the Ideology of Advanced Industrial Society* (London: Routledge, 2002).

6

Liquidating Aesthetics: Brecht

The title of this lecture is 'Liquidating Aesthetics'. That's a terrible phrase, isn't it? 'The Liquidation of Aesthetics' might be better. It's the title of an article by Brecht, which appears in the volume on your reading list, *Brecht on Theatre*, edited by John Willett.[1] As I said to you in a previous lecture, I'm not going to try and give a general lecture on Brecht. In fact, I'm not really going to be fair to Brecht at all. I'm going to be partisan, because I'm only going to deal with those aspects of Brecht's theoretical writings which bear on the themes of this lecture series as they've developed so far. I'm going to discuss Brecht's contributions to the debates over realism and modernism or expressionism in art. (As you know, I've tried to avoid calling the modern position 'modernism'.)

Brecht is, of course, the most well-known of what I've called the Marxist modernists – that is, those artists whose commitment to renewal in art is inseparable from their commitment to renewal in theory. [As for] Benjamin, the modernist position for Brecht can be taken in two different ways. On the one hand, he used pastiche and parody of the old forms. On the other hand, he had the ambition to create wholly changed forms.

---

1   More precisely, the article is called 'Shouldn't We Liquidate Aesthetics?'.

You may remember that in the lecture on Lukács, which was one of the very early ones, we mentioned a journal called *Die Linkskurve* (The left curve). I wonder if you remember what this journal was? It was the journal of the Union of Proletarian-Revolutionary Writers, in Germany, in the late '20s, who were devoted to examining the case for Russian *Proletkult* in Germany – that is, under the conditions of advanced capitalist society. You may remember that the debate in this journal was increasingly dominated by Lukács. One of the things that Lukács and other writers did a lot of was denigrating Brecht. From the mid-to-late '20s – that is, of course, just the time of *The Threepenny Opera* – there was this antagonism towards Brecht within the left, led by Lukács.[2] In the 1930s Lukács was in Russia, and Lukács and Stalin developed the concept of socialist realism, which was far to the left of any *Proletkult* argument which had been developed in the '20s or earlier in Russia. Nevertheless, in 1936 a Popular Front journal was established in Moscow. *Die Linkskurve* was already dead – it had died in 1932. In 1936, this Popular Front journal, which I think I have mentioned, called *Das Wort* (The word), was established in Moscow. The contributors were largely the same people who'd been the contributors to *Die Linkskurve* in Germany, earlier in the '20s. Nevertheless, in spite of the fact that these were the people who'd been denigrating Brecht's work, Brecht agreed to be one of the editors of this journal. He was one of three editors – although, of course, Brecht never went to Moscow at this point. Brecht, at the period in which he was the editor of this journal, wrote many articles answering Lukács's charges against him – but the saint that he was, he didn't publish them, because he felt that they would be too damaging to the precarious unity of the Popular Front. You may remember I said something to you about the Popular Front, that it was a very late development

---

2   Brecht's 'play with music', *Die Dreigroschenoper* (*The Threepenny Opera*) (1928) was adapted from a translation by the German writer Elisabeth Hautmann of the eighteenth-century English ballad opera *The Beggar's Opera* (1728), by John Gay, and four ballads by the medieval French poet François Villon. It was first staged on 31 August 1928 at the Theater am Schiffbauerdamm in Berlin. Bertolt Brecht, *The Threepenny Opera*, transl. Ralph Manheim and John Willett (London: Bloomsbury, 2005).

which encouraged the unity of communist and social-democratic parties, which, earlier on, the Russians and the Comintern had prevented from occurring. I suggested that there were many members of the Frankfurt School that felt that the Comintern's position, preventing a Popular Front, had contributed to the success of fascism. Brecht wrote all these articles which were answering Lukács's position, but he desisted from publishing them, even though Lukács was continuing to publish things which criticised him. Nevertheless, these pieces by Brecht have now been published, although not until the 1950s.[3]

In this lecture, I'm going to do three things. First of all, I'm going to examine this argument between Brecht and Lukács. Secondly, I'm going to look again at the relationship between Benjamin and Brecht. You may remember, in the lecture on Benjamin, I said something about Benjamin acting as Brecht's spokesman in the 1930s, and I want to go into that in greater detail. Finally, I want to look at Adorno's criticisms of Brecht, and see what his position was, as his position was very different from Lukács's. Unlike Lukács, Adorno was very sympathetic to what Brecht was trying to do.

First of all, I would like to point out that discussing Brecht's theories of the production and reception of art – that is, his criticisms of the old habits and his plans for an intended reform – is fundamentally different from discussing the other writers we have dealt with so far. The reason for this, of course, is that Brecht is not a sociologist, nor a philosopher. Unlike the others, he did not develop a general theory or typology of the relationship between art and different types of societies, which is what we've been looking at in the cases of the other writers. Brecht, in his theory, concentrated much more on the critique of modes of consumption of art. Unfortunately, in my opinion, he uses Aristotle's *Poetics*, which some of you may have read, to describe this

---

3 The four most important articles by Brecht on Lukács that were written in the '30s but withheld from *Das Wort* are entitled 'Die Essays von Georg Lukács', 'Über den formalistischen Charakter der Realismustheorie', 'Bermerkungen zu einem Aufsatz', and 'Volkstümlichkeit und Realismus'. They were translated into English and published together as Bertolt Brecht, 'Against Georg Lukács', transl. Stuart Hood, *New Left Review* I/84 (March–April 1974), pp. 39–53.

established mode of consuming art which he wanted to criticise.[4] He doesn't consider any other previous aesthetics or sociological theories of art; and in fact, he got his Aristotle completely wrong. As a result, Brecht's theory is concerned with prescribing the kind of reception he is aiming for as an artist, rather than analysing the possibility of such a reception – that is, sociologically. Another way of putting the same criticism is that Brecht tends to overestimate the originality of his own innovations, some of which were and are the aim of any modernism – which is not to say that Brecht's position isn't distinct, but in some cases he exaggerates his uniqueness. Of course, as an artist and as a poet, Brecht was the most original and creative of them all. But, at the moment, we're just restricting ourselves to his theory.

I want to go into this debate between Brecht and Lukács. You may remember we discussed Lukács's notion of realism – especially his notion of bourgeois realism – and, in fact, we've already looked at the criticisms of this notion, which were made by Bloch, for example. You may remember that by bourgeois realism – realism, that is, in the bourgeois novel – Lukács understood novels which present people as essentially social and political beings which are formed by their society, and which are striving to attain understanding of its contradictions in order to act on them. Texts written in this tradition are rooted in identifiable space and time, and they represent the complex tissue of the interaction of the hero with his social environment. They are universal and concrete, by which he meant typical and harmonious. Such texts present the real possibilities of people, not their abstract imaginings. It was on the basis of this concept of bourgeois realism that Lukács developed a concept of socialist realism. Socialist realism, according to Lukács, would also portray 'rounded' and 'harmonious' characters 'from the inside . . . whose energies are devoted to the building of a different future, and whose psychological and moral makeup is determined by this ambition'.[5] He really extrapolated a

---

4   See Aristotle, *Poetics*, transl. Malcolm Heath (London: Penguin, 1996).

5   Georg Lukács, *Wider den missverstandenen Realismus* – translated with omissions as *Realism in Our Time*, transl. John and Necke Mander (New York: Harper & Row, 1964), pp. 95–6.

notion of socialist realism from what he considered to be the great classics of bourgeois realism.

Brecht was very opposed to this position of Lukács's. He thought that his notion of realism was hidebound and restricted. He considered that it was illegitimate to extrapolate from bourgeois realism to form a concept of socialist realism – that it was an ahistorical and formal way to go about it. Brecht believed that Lukács was reinforcing all the ideas that Brecht considered the modernist must expose and undermine. Lukács's view simply amounted to a restatement of the very aesthetics which Brecht wanted to liquidate, especially Lukács's idea that characterisation in novels or drama should be based on the creation of harmonious individuals. Brecht thought that this was merely inviting the audience to participate vicariously and passively in their overcoming of social contradictions which these characters were engaged in. Instead, according to Brecht, dramatisation should dissolve and break down such lazy habits in the spectator by presenting social reality in a way which accentuates 'the contradictions between everyday appearance and what is historically possible and realisable'.[6] This dramatisation should aim to reveal the strangeness of what passes for normality. It should also reveal the process of the production of that normality, or its formation. As an example of this, Brecht referred to his own use of montage – that is, various ways which involved using new techniques and technology of juxtaposing reality and fiction in order to expose both the traditional illusions of fiction and the illusions of social reality. So, for example, Brecht used film and photography on stage; he interrupted action, and so on. Brecht called this a 'realism for his time'. He considered that there was no one way of being a realist, which is what Lukács's position implied. Instead, if one was going to be a consistent realist, it would be necessary for the artist to be constantly vigilant, for it was necessary to change what counts as realism as society and social reality change.

Lukács had a reply to this position of Brecht's. He said, just as Brecht said of him, that Brecht's position was formal; that it resulted

---

6   Eugene Lunn, 'Marxism and Art in the Era of Stalin and Hitler: The Brecht–Lukács Debate', *New German Critique* 3 (1974), p. 15.

in artificial construction of reality, which would be unrecognisable to the audience, and that instead of politicising them, it would paralyse them. Brecht, in his turn, had an answer to Lukács. He explicated further his notion of the theatre of the 'smoker' or 'thinker'. He thought that people should smoke in the theatre – which is something, you notice, I don't encourage in my lectures . . . He thought that if people were encouraged to smoke, drink, chat, in the theatre, that this would help the development of the kind of realism that he wanted. I think his notion of realism is really extremely cerebral. By realism he meant 'discovering the causal complexes of society/ unmasking the prevailing view of things as the view of those who rule it/writing from the standpoint of the class which offers the broadest solutions for the pressing difficulties in which human society is caught/emphasising the element of development/making possible the concrete, and making possible abstractions from it'.[7] Now, Brecht was well aware – and, in this sense, he could answer Lukács's position – that some forms of expressionism and modernism had merely reinforced the old evils, instead of breaking them – which, as you may remember from the lecture on Lukács, was Lukács's basic criticism of most forms of modernism in art: that they merely colluded in distortion instead of analysing it or breaking it. Brecht, too, considered that some forms of expressionism were self-indulgent. In fact, in his own works, as I suggested at the beginning, he tended to oscillate between pastiche and parody of old forms – an example of that would be *The Threepenny Opera* – and the attempt to create wholly changed dramatic forms – his platform plays and *Lehrstücke*.[8] In fact, Adorno was more critical of the second than the first.

Now I'd like to go on to look at Benjamin's attempt to provide a sociological analysis to underpin Brecht's notion of epic theatre. Benjamin tried both to explain what Brecht meant by 'epic theatre', and also to take the sociological analysis underlying it further than

---

7   Brecht, 'Against Georg Lukács', p. 50.

8   The *Lehrstücke* ('learning-plays') were an experimental form of theatre developed by Brecht in the 1920s and '30s, which emphasise learning through acting and a dissolution of the distinction between actor and audience.

Brecht had taken it himself. Benjamin considered that you couldn't really assess whether a work of art was reactionary or revolutionary by reading off its content – that is, by asking what the position of a work of art is vis-à-vis the relationships of production, by asking whether the content of a work of art is revolutionary or reactionary. Instead, Benjamin thought that you have to ask the question: What is the function of a work of art *within* the relations of production? It's only if you ask that question, rather than the question of its position vis-à-vis the relations of production, [that you can] enquire into the question of the form of a work of art – what Benjamin called its 'technique'. He was interested in providing a sociological analysis of the form of a work of art, rather than reading off political implications from its content. This, by the way, is stated in his famous article 'The Author as Producer', which is in the book on the reading list called *Understanding Brecht*.[9] Some of you might have read it. In this article, Benjamin uses examples of revolutionary form by analysing the relationship of the artist to society in Russia – a society which, at the time he was writing, was engaged in the task of building socialism. He contrasted the attempts to develop a revolutionary form in Russia, which he thought should be emulated in a capitalist society, with *Neue Sachlichkeit* in capitalist Germany. Do you remember at the beginning I broke down modernism into expressionism, *Proletkult*, *Neue Sachlichkeit*, and Surrealism? Benjamin was particularly interested in *Neue Sachlichkeit*. He pointed out that this was a kind of art which had had revolutionary aims in the first place, but which had been co-opted by the capitalist class – that is, *Neue Sachlichkeit* had originally been subversive, but it had come to supply the production apparatus instead of changing it. Benjamin said that the result of this form of art was to turn '*the struggle against misery into an object of consumption*'.[10]

If one was an artist in a capitalist society, how could one avoid having one's art co-opted in this way, having its originally revolutionary aims subverted? Benjamin said that it was necessary to

---

9   Walter Benjamin, 'The Author as Producer', in *Understanding Brecht*, transl. Anna Bostock (London: Verso, 2003), pp. 85–104.

10   Ibid., p. 96. Emphasis in original.

demonstrate solidarity with the proletariat, not only in the mind, but as a producer of works.[11] What did he mean by this? What really is the force of this distinction? I don't think he was very successful in establishing its force. He took up Brecht's concept of epic theatre as a notion of art which would demonstrate solidarity with the proletariat not merely in the mind, but as a producer. He considered this concept of epic art to be a didactic art which prescribes a new attitude. It would transform the writer from a supplier of the production apparatus into what Benjamin called 'an engineer who sees his task in adapting that apparatus to the ends of the proletarian revolution'.[12] Benjamin had a notion of the artist as the engineer.

Epic theatre – and this is Brecht's concept of epic theatre, which Benjamin was recapitulating – is contrasted with traditional dramatic theatre. Epic theatre is a different form of narrative from dramatic theatre. It involves storytelling, action which is quoted or recalled, spoken by the characters in the play as if they were speaking in the third person. Plays of this kind present the determining social factors of the action, which should be shown as alterable. The spectators should be divided by the action according to their class position. This would be accomplished by plays which contain pointed sketch-like situations, songs, and choruses, addressed directly to the audience, thread-like dramaturgy, loosely linking scenes and songs. It would use technical advances and technological advances to stress the reportage aspect. Now, I've got a quote here from Brecht which contrasts the experience which the dramatic theatre's spectator would have in the theatre with the experience which the epic theatre's spectator would have in the theatre: 'The dramatic theatre's spectator says: Yes, I have felt like that too. – Just like me. – It's only natural. – It'll never change. – The sufferings of this man appal me, because they're inescapable. – That's great art; it all seems the most obvious thing in the world. – I weep when they weep, I laugh when they laugh.' Now, by contrast with this view: 'The epic theatre's spectator says: I'd never have thought it. – That's not the way. – That's extraordinary, hardly

---

11   See ibid., p. 91.
12   Ibid, p. 102.

believable. – It's got to stop. – The sufferings of this man appal me, because they are unnecessary. – That's great art: nothing obvious in it. – I laugh when they weep, I weep when they laugh.'[13]

As I said, Benjamin endorsed this notion of epic theatre as a kind of modernist art which would not be subverted or co-opted in the way that he thought, and Brecht thought too, other forms of modernism had been subverted and co-opted by being developed within a capitalist society, rather than within a society like Russia, which they considered to be, at that point, a socialist society. I think that this analysis is really quite inconsistent, because, in spite of this analysis of what you might call 'repressive toleration' . . . I don't know if you know that idea. It's Marcuse's phrase, and it's one of the many things that Marcuse took from the earlier Frankfurt School. Do you know this phrase, 'repressive toleration'? Have you come across it? No. Okay. Well, repressive toleration is a phrase which Marcuse developed much later, in the '60s, to mean that a capitalist society is quite capable of tolerating antagonistic cultural forms. In fact, it has an interest in so doing. For example, the so-called counterculture, which first of all had subversive and revolutionary intentions, eventually becomes commercialised, and part of the structure of consumption in a capitalist society. Marcuse extended this idea to cover lots of things. I'm saying that Benjamin's analysis of the way in which *Neue Sachlichkeit*'s originally revolutionary intentions were subverted by capitalist society is very close to the notion of what Marcuse developed later on in *Eros and Civilisation* – or *One-Dimensional Man*, perhaps . . . It's very similar to Marcuse's notion of repressive toleration, what he also called 'repressive desublimation'.[14] That is, things that look, in a capitalist society, as

13   Brecht, 'Theatre for Pleasure or Theatre for Instruction', in *Brecht on Theatre: The Development of an Aesthetic*, ed. and transl. John Willet (London: Eyre Methuen, 1964), pp. 69–77.

14   Herbert Marcuse developed his theory of 'repressive desublimation' in his work *One-Dimensional Man: Studies in the Ideology of Advanced Industrial Society* (London: Routledge, 2002 [1964]), pp. 59–86. He then reformulated it as 'repressive tolerance' in an essay of that title included in the volume *Critique of Pure Tolerance* (1965), co-written with Robert Wolff and Barrington Moore (Boston, MA: Beacon, 1965), pp. 81–118.

if they're liberating, are in fact a new form of repression, once they've been taken over by the dominant apparatuses. It seems to me inconsistent that, on the one hand, Benjamin pointed out so clearly the way in which *Neue Sachlichkeit* had been subverted within Germany in the 1920s and had become, as he says, an 'object of consumption', and, [on the other hand], the way he was so sanguine that epic theatre would not be perverted in a capitalist society. Of course, Adorno's argument was that epic theatre was just as perverted by the dominant relations of distribution and consumption of art as *Neue Sachlichkeit* and other forms of expressionism. You may remember, from last week, Adorno's concept of the culture industry, which was precisely designed to criticise ideas like this of Benjamin's. I think, in this particular essay, Benjamin was translating, far too readily, the experience of Russia to [the] conditions of Germany.

The other problem with this view of Benjamin's, this interpretation of Brecht, is that many of the so-called epic changes are not really unique to Brecht. Both Benjamin and Brecht overlooked the similarities between Brecht's programme and other forms of modernism. These other forms of modernism – there are all sorts of people here, from Kafka, Joyce, Thomas Mann, as well as our Marxist modernists – did not put so much emphasis on the aspect of prescribing these changes. Both Brecht and Benjamin put a lot of emphasis on the fact that these changes were to be prescribed or taught. Nevertheless, many other forms of modernism can be seen as having the same aims, but they tried to achieve them more indirectly.

Finally, I'd like to discuss Adorno's criticisms of Brecht. Adorno, unlike Lukács, was a very sympathetic critic of Brecht's. He sympathised with Brecht's intention, which I mentioned earlier on, to create a realism for our time. He wasn't at all on Lukács's side of that. He reviewed *The Threepenny Opera* with great enthusiasm when it was first produced, although he stressed in it the use of pastiche and parody of the old forms, and not the exploiting of new techniques which create a wholly changed dramatic form.[15] Adorno wrote an

15   Gillian Rose, *The Melancholy Science: An Introduction to the Thought of Theodor W. Adorno* (London: Verso, 2014), p. 165.

essay after the war called 'The Difficulties of Composing'.[16] It was a companion piece to a famous essay by Brecht called 'Five Difficulties of Writing the Truth'.[17] This was an essay by Brecht written in 1934, and it concerned the difficulties of writing the truth under the conditions of a fascist dictatorship. The five difficulties, according to Brecht, were (i) having the courage to write the truth, (ii) having the cleverness to recognise the truth, (iii) having the artistic ability to make the truth manipulable like a weapon, (iv) having the judgement to choose those in whose hands the truth would become effective, and (v) having the cunning to spread the truth amongst the masses. Adorno echoed these five difficulties in his article on composing music. Why I'm pointing this out is to stress that Adorno, like Brecht, wrote as an artist – from the point of view of the artist – on the difficulties of circumventing existing consciousness, and the traditional concept of the subject and dramatic collusion. But, although Adorno wrote as an artist, unlike Benjamin and Brecht he also went much more into the sociological question of how art might be received, however revolutionary its intentions. As you know, he developed this notion of the culture industry which stressed that you had to look at the intervening mechanisms between the production of art and its distribution or consumption in a capitalist society, an aspect which Benjamin and Brecht tended to simplify.

Adorno, like Brecht, aimed as an artist and as a theorist to undermine and change existing consciousness by attending to the form of the work of art – that is, to the relationship between the structuring of meaning in a work and how that meaning might be received or distorted in a capitalist society. But Adorno came to differ radically from Brecht as to how a radical restructuring might be achieved. Adorno argued that Brecht's attempt to re-educate the audience failed. Why did it fail? As we've said earlier on, Brecht set out to

16   Theodor W. Adorno, 'Difficulties', transl. Susan H. Gillespie, in *Essays on Music*, ed. Richard Leppert (Berkeley: University of California Press, 2002), pp. 644–80.

17   Bertolt Brecht, 'Five Difficulties in Writing the Truth', transl. Laura Bradley and Tom Kuhn, in *Brecht on Art and Politics*, ed. Tom Kuhn and Steve Giles (London: Metheun, 2003), pp. 141–56.

eliminate the traditional concept of character, and he felt that Lukács's notion of character was really a very traditional one. But what Brecht put in the place of the traditional concept of character was, or amounted to, according to Adorno, the establishing of another set of unintended and equally undesirable illusions in the place of the ones destroyed. Adorno considered – and he was considering Brecht's plays as much as his theory, or rather the relationship between the two – that there were contradictions between Brecht's practice and his theories. He thought that Brecht in his plays did not succeed in making social reality look strange – in showing the strangeness of what passes for normality – or dissolving that normality. Instead, Adorno argued, Brecht had simply made social reality look straightforward, and that this was to create a new and pernicious fiction that social reality really is simple and transparent. What's more, Adorno believed that Brecht had ratified this new and pernicious illusion, or made it even more pernicious, by stating it in a coercive and dictatorial fiction – that is, Brecht and Benjamin's attempt to prescribe a new attitude.

Adorno went on to analyse why he thought these thoughts had arisen, or why Brecht had failed in his attempt to re-educate the audience. It depends on his concept of the culture industry as we discussed it last week. He considered that Brecht had attempted a direct escape from the old illusions – a too-direct escape from the old illusions – instead of undermining them on their own ground. Another way of putting this is that Brecht had tried to create a wholly changed dramatic form which would have no relationship to the earlier forms which were implicated in the old social relations. But because he'd attempted to create something so utterly different, he was therefore able only to have a very external effect on the old, entrenched meanings which he wanted to counteract. Another way of putting the same point is that Brecht underestimated the power of prevailing consciousness, and of the social institutions which determined that consciousness. He overestimated the likelihood of the success of a revolutionary art considered outside the social relations which were determining the position of that art in a society. He didn't consider, for example, that the audience might continue to consume or receive the new works of art in the old ways. For example, many people, many left-wing people, were rather appalled by the immense success of *The Threepenny Opera* in Berlin, because the audience consisted of the very classes which were meant to be devastated by the opera – which were being criticised by it.

The underlying argument which Adorno was developing was that, in a capitalist society, it is impossible for a work of art to guarantee its own effect. You cannot write a work of art with the aim of guaranteeing or ensuring a specific social effect or a specific function. There will always be intervening mechanisms which are determined by the other social institutions in that society – institutions of power, authority, ideology – which will intervene and complicate the reception of the work of art. In such a society, to try and commandeer dramaturgy, as Brecht did, would result in him achieving quite the opposite of what he wanted to achieve. Brecht wished to destroy bourgeois autonomous art. You may remember that we discussed the concept of autonomous art in the lecture on Benjamin – that it was Benjamin who precisely showed that autonomy is itself socially determined in a capitalist society. Both Brecht and Benjamin considered that the new technical and technological changes would destroy the old autonomous art and create a new functional art – that is, an art whose relationship to politics would be direct. Adorno argued that, on the contrary, Brecht had made art even more autonomous by using it didactically – by emphasising the primacy of lesson over form. Thus, the basic underlying criticism is that Brecht had not armed himself effectively against the old illusions and the old powers.

That's really all I have for today. In next week's lecture, I'm going to say much more about Adorno and Marcuse's position on all these things. In a sense, I'm going to give Adorno and Marcuse the last word.

The Search for Style:
Adorno; Kafka or Mann?

You may have noticed that, in the other lectures, I've tended to argue that, on the issue of realism versus modernism or – well, we never decided what to call modernism, but let's take the easy way out for now – I believe Adorno's position to be the most sociologically consistent. What I mean by that is that, unlike Lukács, Bloch, Benjamin, and Brecht (to a certain extent, although it's not really fair to bring Brecht in on this), Adorno applied his generalisation of Marx's theory of commodity fetishism to every stage of production, exchange, distribution, and reception of artworks. You may remember that, in the other lectures, I've argued that the others weren't consistent in doing this. Adorno didn't assume, as all the others did in one way or another, that the relationship between the production and reception of art in advanced capitalist society would be undistorted by intervening mechanisms – that is, mechanisms of commodity fetishism, turning art into commodities.

We have discussed already three aspects of Adorno's thought. We've discussed his notion of the culture industry – that is, how new mechanisms of distribution of art in late-capitalist society alter the meaning of that art. We've discussed as well Adorno's criticisms of Benjamin and Brecht – that is, his criticisms of the attempt to use art politically in an instrumental or functional way. His criticism was that this aim would be inherently self-defeating under the conditions of commodity relations. We've also discussed Adorno's criticisms of Lukács and Bloch – of their argument that the fascist period was one of disintegration. On the contrary, Adorno and Horkheimer saw that period as one of consolidation of new forms of social control that would persist in advanced capitalist society even after the defeat of fascism. That was the discussion of *Dialectic of Enlightenment*.

Today, I want to try and put Adorno's position more positively, to show that Adorno developed a systematic Marxist sociology of art, and to show that this sociology of art was equally capable of being critical of so-called modernist (or avant-garde) art as it was of popular art. (Adorno was actually critical of this split, but he was, equally, critical of both kinds of art which the split had produced.) I also want to try and show, in the last section of this lecture, how Adorno's position influences the detailed analysis of literary texts. He was particularly concerned (as was Lukács) with Kafka and Mann. I'm taking up literature here, but I'm also going to say something early on about music. All these theories, Adorno applied both to music and to literature. My claim is that Adorno developed a systematic Marxist sociology of art – more systematic and more consistent than anybody else that we've looked at in this lecture series.

Adorno thought that 'avant-garde' was the wrong name, because one of the things that was characteristic of the so-called 'avant' in twentieth-century art was that it did not lead a 'garde' – if you see what I mean. Adorno wanted to explain this. The phrase 'avant-garde' is quite inaccurate – but anyway, I'll use it for the moment. Adorno insisted that so-called avant-garde art and popular art should be examined in relationship to each other since – and this is a famous quotation; I've probably said it ten times, I can't remember – 'both are torn halves of an integral freedom to which, however, they do not add up.' (Have I said that before? Yes? Good.) In his sociology of music and literature, and in his aesthetic theory, Adorno used materialist concepts to examine the relationships of the torn halves, systematically, centred on the theory of commodity fetishism. I'm going to quote from a letter that Adorno wrote to a friend. You can see what personal letters he wrote . . . This is from Adorno to the composer

Ernst Krenek – I don't know if some of you have heard of Ernst Krenek.[1]

> The commodity character of music is not determined by its being exchanged, but by its being *abstractly* exchanged [this is very closely following on from that chapter of Marx's in *Captial*] in the way in which Marx explained the commodity form: hence not an immediate but a 'reified' exchange relation occurs. When you [Krenek] explain the art 'has become autonomous' as the decisive change, that is really what I mean by its commodity character.[2]

You may remember that Benjamin and Adorno both thought that the notion of autonomy in art was itself socially determined – unlike Lukács, who felt that once society intervened in art, art's autonomy was destroyed. Adorno went on to say:

> Only it is the same phenomenon described not from the side of the *relations* of production, but from the side of the *forces* of production ... If by capitalism one understands more than mere 'for money', namely, [one understands] the *totality* of the social process defined as a unity of exchange by abstract labour time, then, in an exact sense, capitalism has made art into a commodity *together with* men.[3]

Now, I'm going to try and explain this intimate letter. Adorno is stressing the abstract nature of the exchange of cultural commodities, in opposition to the perspective put forward by Krenek, which was very similar to that of Benjamin. First, he means that the relation which results from the exchange and the concomitant consumption of what is exchanged is not an immediate or intelligible one. This is

---

1   Ernst Krenek (1900–1991) was an Austrian, then American, modernist composer and writer.

2   Adorno to Krenek, 30 September 1932, in *Theodor W. Adorno und Ernst Krenef Briefwechsel*, ed. Wolfgang Rogge (Frankfurt am Mein: Suhrkamp, 1974), p. 36. Rose's translation. Interjections in squared brackets are Rose's own.

3   Ibid.

very similar to Marx's point. Marx contrasted the intelligibility of exchange in non-commodity-producing societies – that is, feudal society – with its unintelligibility in capitalist society. Marx said that social relations can be understood by people in societies which don't produce commodities, but in commodity-producing societies, social relationships become unintelligible to people. Where music is concerned, the illusion that exchange and consumption is intelligible is particularly strong due to its apparent immediate value in use. (I'm going to repeat that grotesque sentence and then give you an example. It's a very simple point, actually). *Where music is concerned, the illusion that exchange and consumption is intelligible is particularly strong due to its apparently immediate value in use.* Music has an apparently immediate value in use, which means no more than when you buy a record and you put it on a gramophone and rave to it or something, you can enjoy it immediately. It seems to have an immediate value in use. Adorno is arguing that, because music can be enjoyed in this way, even when you're actually buying a commodity, a record, this particularly obscures the fact that that record is a commodity. That's what that cumbersome sentence means.

In the second case, this notion of the abstract nature of exchange is emphasised by Adorno as the premise for examining any other features of the relationship between society and music – for example, production, reproduction, and consumption. Adorno thought that this approach would do more justice to the objective conditions of subjective modes of reception of art. Adorno always denied, as any good sociologist would, that what we consider to be subjective in our reception of works of art really is subjective in some sort of ultimate, reductive, idiosyncratic sense. Subjectivity, for any sociologist, is always socially determined. Adorno wanted to show that the most subjective responses to works of art can be shown to be systematically determined by the social structure. Adorno was trying to escape from Krenek's too-simple view that art is distorted – that is very much near Lukács's view as well – by being incorporated into the processes of capitalism, or from Benjamin's view that an enlightened consciousness would triumph from the immediate effects of new technology. He was opposing both of these views.

Adorno's sociology of art is based on the notion that a new contradiction has developed. His examination of music and literature is devoted to examining genres and individual works of art in the light of the thesis that a contradiction has developed between the forces and relations of production. That's a very standard Marxist point, isn't it, that social change occurs when new forces of production come into old established relations of production? You probably know that from your reading of Marx. Now, Adorno wanted to say that a contradiction has developed in modern art, and he used Marx's categories. He said that a contradiction has developed between the forces and relations of production, but, of course, he means the forces and relations of *artistic* production, not manufacturing production – which is, of course, what Marx meant. So, this was a deliberately provocative way to put it, on Adorno's part.

On the one hand, there will always be a disjunction between production and consumption of art in a society based on the production of commodities – that is, under the conditions which produce so-called autonomous art – for the criterion of artistic production or composition that a work is authentic or unique, will always be more or less at odds with the demands of consumption or reception that it should be intelligible. This distinction between the authenticity or uniqueness of a work and its need to be intelligible is a very general dichotomy which Adorno thinks all art falls into.

On the other hand, in the present age, he thinks a very special contradiction has arisen. I'm going to quote from him. 'In the present age' – by which he means the twentieth century in general, I suppose – 'the contradiction between the forces of production and the relations of production becomes flagrant: the forces of production are displaced into high, quasi-privileged spheres, isolated, and therefore, even when they incorporate true consciousness, are also partly false. The lower spheres obey the predominant relations of production.'[4] As an example of this, he was thinking of the music of Berg, Webern, Schoenberg, but also of the work of Kafka and Thomas Mann. The

---

4   Theodor W. Adorno, *Introduction to the Sociology of Music*, transl. E. B. Ashton (New York: Seabury, 1989), p. 225. Rose's translation.

'lower spheres', by which he means popular art or popular culture, obey the predominant relations of production.

This contradiction is derived from the prevalent mode of exchange which, combined with new forms of distribution (that is, the kind of reproduction that Benjamin was interested in), results in a dislocation of the realm of culture. But this notion of contradiction taken from Marx is very odd. It implies displacement between production and consumption which determines the status quo but does not change it, and which appears to be a permanent rather than an inherently unstable situation. Marx's notion of displacement was developed to explain social change. Adorno seems to be developing a notion of social contradiction to explain why *nothing* is changing.

The notion of forces of production and the notion of relations of production are not really commensurable. By 'forces of production', Adorno means a specialist skill of composition (whether for the market or not), and techniques and technology which both determine the tools of composition. He does not refer to the general preconditions of buying and selling labour-power or of the labour process in general – that is, he doesn't anchor his analysis in a general examination of social institutions outside the world of art. But by 'relations of production' in art, Adorno means something approaching the conventional Marxist notion, namely: lifestyles and habits of consumption; consciousness shared and differentiated according to class position.

Now, you may remember, as an example of these general ideas, we discussed in an earlier lecture what Adorno meant by the 'culture industry'. In fact, what I've just explicated is another way of putting his 'culture industry' thesis. You may remember – again, I'm going to stick to music for the moment, but I'll be switching to literature in a minute – that Adorno wanted to link up in a technical sense this idea of Marx's that, in a capitalist society which produces commodities, social relations become unintelligible, with the question of intelligibility or unintelligibility in works of art. For example, if you hear a piece of music by Schoenberg, you may feel that you don't understand it. Now, Adorno wanted to link that feeling that people have when they hear a piece of music by Schoenberg – that they don't understand it – to the lack of understanding which people generally have in a society which is based on commodity fetishism. You remember the initial definition of commodity fetishism? Social relations between people appear in the form of relationships between things. Adorno wanted to establish a link between the ways in which popular art seemed so immediately intelligible to us – whereas the avant-garde (such as Schoenberg) seems so difficult to understand – and the illusions, produced by commodity fetishism, that society is simply understandable when it isn't, or that it's unintelligible when it is in fact intelligible. (I don't know if I've got that right, but never mind . . .) That's one of the reasons that I think his sociology of art is so interesting. He manages to make this connection which neither Lukács, nor Benjamin, nor Bloch managed to make.

I'll just remind you how it worked out in music. You may remember that Adorno offers a more technical exposition of the notion that the meaning of music may be altered in the medium of reproduction – that is, when music is performed in the concert hall or broadcast on the radio. This exposition depends on the contrast between the technical notion of intelligibility established by classical music and the different norm of intelligibility which tends to be demanded when music is received by the untrained ear. In music, unlike literature, it's quite easy to make a distinction between the type of intelligibility – by which I mean the sort of things that you'll be able to understand if you've had a training in music and the sort of things you'll tend to look for if you listen to, say, Mozart or Bach or Beethoven, if you haven't had an education in music. (I don't know if my music friends here would agree with me. They'll doubtless tell me afterwards, but anyway.) That was Adorno's position: that you could make a distinction between the different kinds of intelligibility that people would demand in music according to whether they'd been trained or not. (I suppose Adorno would make the same distinction in relation to other arts, where the difference would depend not so much on whether you'd been trained or not, but certainly on whether you'd had certain kinds of education.) Adorno's argument was that music is adjusted at the stage of reproduction, whether its classical music or pop music, in order to attain the greatest intelligibility to people who listen to it with an untrained ear, which may amount to the least intelligibility in the first sense – that is, in the classically trained sense.

What I wanted to go on to say before we go on to literature is that Adorno didn't only analyse so-called popular music or the popularising of music. I think we did discuss that in a previous lecture. He also analysed so-called 'new music'. 'New music' is another one of these thousands of phrases we've had for modern art. It refers to the work of the first and second Vienna School, particularly Schoenberg, Berg, and Webern. Adorno considered that this music was composed on the basis of new techniques which were designed to avoid the predominant modes of distribution; yet such music, owing to its esoteric nature, was fated to display 'the same disastrous pattern' which it sought to combat.[5] Adorno's thesis is that some kinds of critical response to society, whether in art or in politics or in philosophy or almost anything, will in fact merely reproduce in another form the very thing which they're trying to fight. (I don't know if that's a new idea to you. Have you ever thought about that? You may have done. It may be banal . . . It's a genuine question. I'll say it again.) Many forms of radical activity – whether artistic, political, social, theoretical – are fated to display 'the same disastrous pattern' which they seek to combat. Adorno thought that, because such a contradiction had developed between popular music and, say, new music, because of these developments in the mode of distribution of art – the mechanical reproduction which Benjamin was interested in – even that art which he thought was most genuinely radical and critical ended up displaying the same disastrous patterns which it was trying to fight against. Adorno was equally critical of so-called avantgarde art or modernist art or expressionist art as he was of popular art. You may remember, by contrast, that Lukács tended to debase all modern art, and that Bloch tended to embrace it. Adorno's position is

---

5   Rose takes this phrase from Adorno's *Minima Moralia*: 'And how comfortless is the thought that the sickness of the normal does not necessarily imply as its opposite the health of the sick, but that the latter usually only presents, in a different way, the same disastrous pattern.' Theodor W. Adorno, *Minima Moralia: Reflections on a Damaged Life*, transl. E. F. N. Jephcott (London: Verso, 2005), p. 60.

a third one. He tries to show that expressionist or modernist art or new music (all these thousands of phrases), although he could give them a genuinely radical role, that they too were bound to fall into some of the same contradictions as art which adapts. Art which adapts and art which resists adaptation to the new modes of mechanical reproduction is all fated to display this pattern.

Adorno explained a bit more what he means by this contradiction. He argued that the overall function of music in society has changed, and that this change affects every aspect of music. Music has lost its previous autonomy. This autonomy was determined by the emancipation of music from an immediate context of use and ritual and its acquiring value in exchange. That's very much like Benjamin's position. The result was music which partly legitimised the social order which produced it, and which partly criticised that order. By contrast, the breach between these functions of music – that is, music which legitimises and criticises at the same time – has become complete. They are completely separated now. He's saying that, earlier on in capitalism, the function of legitimising social order and of criticising it could occur in the same piece of music, but that now it's different kinds of music which does each of these things. Some kinds of music legitimise the social structure. Adorno called these totally 'functionalised' kinds of music.[6] For example, music for distraction or diversion – entertainment. While music which has a critical function has become so far removed from general reception – that is, from what we can generally understand – that it no longer exercises an effective critical role. There are only very few people who can appreciate Schoenberg's music. Even if it is a genuinely radical music, it's going to be so divorced from general reception that it will no longer be effectively critical. An illusion of immediacy in use, and hence of intelligibility, surrounds the reception of totally functionalised music: that is, people think that music which diverts or distracts them is simply intelligible, it can be understood immediately, whereas Adorno says that it can't. Similarly, that music which has become very removed from people's understanding is not as unintelligible as it seems.

---

6   Adorno, *Introduction to the Sociology of Music*, pp. 39–54.

Where both music and literature are concerned, Adorno argued that the modernist position is as inherently self-defeating, and is as full of contradictions, as any popular music or art, and as Brecht or Benjamin's idea of a new functional art. He worked this out in relation, most of all, to music – that is, Schoenberg, Berg, and Webern.

I now want to go on to discuss this position in relation to literature. Where literature is concerned, Adorno didn't examine, on the one hand, avant-garde literature, and on the other hand, popular literature – which would have been the consistent thing to do, since, where music is concerned, he examined popular music and avant-garde music. Where literature is concerned, he only really examined what you'd call avant-garde art. (I actually have a student at the moment who's doing a DPhil and is going to try and apply this notion of looking at popular art in relationship to avant-garde art to literature.) For now, we're just going to compare Adorno's position with Lukács's on analysing Kafka and Mann, and see how their different positions affect the understanding and analysis of specific texts. (How many of you are engaged in reading Kafka and Mann? Some of you are. Yes. Well, this won't be a revision session, I promise you, if you're taking your exams next term . . .)

You may remember – but I will remind you of it – Lukács's distinction between realism and modernism. In the last lecture, which was, unfortunately, some time ago now, we recapitulated what Lukács said on realism. You may remember that, under 'modernism', Lukács lumped several movements together. I've tried to keep away from that, not entirely successfully . . . By 'modernism' – and this is covering all sorts of different points of view – Lukács interpreted everyone: Joyce, Brecht, Kafka . . . In fact, Thomas Mann was almost the only twentieth-century writer who he didn't consider a modernist. Lukács considered that modernist texts were based on the view that man is, by nature, solitary, asocial, and unable to enter into relationships with other human beings. The modernist hero is not concerned with understanding social reality or acting on it. Texts of this kind portray individuals ' "thrown-into-the world", meaninglessly, unfathomably', without any development of personality, and hence statically, and ahistorically.[7] (We've been through this before. I'm just reminding you of what he said.) Such texts, such writings, concentrate on the abstract potentials of an individual's life: his rich imaginings, which are preferred to social realities. It is thus, according to Lukács, intensely subjective literature, which colludes in the distortion of reality instead of fighting it, by its obsession with styles to convey such subjective experience. Lukács was very opposed to experiment in style, and he couldn't give it any sociological or radical interpretation.

Kafka's work is, for Lukács, the prototype of modernist art. Its techniques betray a view of man terrified in the presence of 'utterly strange and hostile reality', and reduced to 'total impotence [and] paralysis in the face of the unintelligible power of circumstance'.[8] This essentially subjective vision is identified with reality itself. Kafka's description of the world serves the end of presenting 'an allegory of transcendent Nothingness'.[9] Kafka uses a wealth of naturalistic detail to convey a fragmented world, and personal horror and impotence, but his details – you'll see that Lukács couldn't deny the fact that, in some senses, Kafka's texts are very naturalistic and descriptive – 'are not, as in realism, the nodal points of individual or social life; they are cryptic symbols of an unfathomable transcendence. The stronger their evocative power, the deeper is the abyss, the more evident the allegorical gap between meaning and existence.'[10] This is Lukács's grand condemnation of Kafka. He's basically saying that Kafka is socially irresponsible, if you haven't got the point.

According to Lukács, Thomas Mann, on the other hand, deals quite differently with distortion in society. Lukács approved of Thomas Mann. The settings of Thomas Mann's novels, according to Lukács, are 'free from transcendental reference',[11] and his characterisation of

---

7   Georg Lukács, 'The Ideology of Modernism', in *The Meaning of Contemporary Realism*, transl. John and Necke Mander (London: Merlin, 1969), p. 21.

8   Georg Lukács, *Realism in Our Time*, transl. John and Necke Mander (New York: Harper & Row, 1964), p. 36.

9   Ibid., p. 53.

10   Ibid., p. 78.

11   Ibid.

individuals is based on his desire to probe 'into the complexity of present-day reality'.[12] In fact, Lukács makes Thomas Mann sound like a really dull sociologist. These individuals in Mann's texts represent different aspects of the whole. Mann made the insight that the artist is one of the main mediators of people's experience of the 'underworld of the human mind' and of social reality into the object of many of his books, from *Tonio Kröger* to *Doctor Faustus*, not by stylistic experimentation, like the modernists did, but by 'increasingly rigorous studies of the problem in its social context'.[13] *Doctor Faustus*, according to Lukács, is the apogee of such treatment. (I hope some of you realise how peculiar all this is, because *Doctor Faustus* is really the most modernist of modernist books – but Lukács thought it was a classic realist text.) Within this novel, *Doctor Faustus* – this will make sense, I'm afraid, only to those of you who've read it – two perspectives are contained, according to Lukács: that of Faust, the composer Adrian Leverkühn, the musician who inhabits the small world of the isolated artist; and that of the narrator, Serenus Zeitblom, who is located in strictly observed social and historical time. As a result, a 'rounded' realistic novel is created on the theme of examining 'the tragedy of modern art'.[14] The tragedy is that, while the artist knows that his stylistic problems are determined by the real historical situation of his culture, he is determined to concede nothing to them, and to work independently of them, thereby creating a highly formal art which is at the same time subjective, 'the concentrated expression of intellectual and moral decadence'.[15] Lukács is basically saying that Thomas Mann shares his own position, that modern art is decadent, and that he wrote a novel in which he showed this decadent artist and surrounded him with a realist commentary.

Adorno disagreed with Lukács on every count: with Lukács's idea of form and style, with Lukács's idea of realism and of modernism,

---

12   Ibid., p. 79.
13   Ibid.
14   Georg Lukács, 'The Tragedy of Modern Art' (1948), in *Essays on Thomas Mann*, transl. Stanley Mitchell (London: Merlin, 1969), pp. 68–9.
15   Ibid., p. 68.

and with his interpretation of the contemporary plight of literature. Lukács, he argues, is unable to understand the stylistic and technical features of the novel, because he subordinates such features to the underlying perspective or view of the world – that is, to the content of a work of art. Because Lukács so much disliked stylistic experimentation, he would only ever concentrate on the content of a work of art. In fact, you may remember from our first lecture, in Lukács's own earlier book, *The Theory of the Novel*, Lukács himself had asked questions about the relationship between the possibility of artistic form in different historical epochs. You may remember, in that very first lecture, I argued that the rest of the Frankfurt School were more consistent than Lukács in taking up some of the themes of this book, *The Theory of the Novel*, turning them against Lukács's later work. This was particularly true of Adorno. Adorno learnt at Lukács's knee, and then, later on, attacked Lukács with Lukács's own ideas, and this one particularly. Lukács is making the definitions of 'modernism' and 'realism' depend on the content of a work of art. Adorno argues that this leads Lukács to interpret style, whether modernist or realist, as a simple reflection of reality, and to describe modernist style in varying biological terms, such as 'decadent' or 'sick', instead of examining the merely apparently invariant atemporal quality of such style.[16] Adorno is quite rightly pointing out that no Marxist or sociologist should interpret anything by calling it 'decadent' or 'sick', because they're biological terms, aren't they?[17] And it's precisely the sociologist or the Marxist task to explain why such ideas arise, and not to use them.

Lukács rebukes modernist novels for their ontological themes of loneliness, isolation, and terror; but, in fact, it's Lukács himself who has made such themes into ontological ones – that is, fixed aspects of the world; I'm using 'ontological' to mean that – by not investigating

---

16   'If it is a question of historical relationships, words like sick and healthy should be avoided altogether. They have nothing to do with the progress/reaction dimension; they are brought in purely for the sake of their demagogic appeal.' Theodor W. Adorno, 'Extorted Reconciliation: On Georg Lukács' *Realism in Our Time*', in *Notes to Literature*, transl. Shierry Weber Nicholsen (New York: Columbia University Press, 1991), vol. 1, p. 221.

17   Etymologically, 'decadent' is linked to 'decay'.

the specific historical and social determination of them. It is Lukács's notion of realism in literature which is fundamentally at fault, for a work of art is not real in the same way that a society is real. Lukács has, in effect, taken the ground away from any radical aesthetics by his naive-realist account of the relationship between art and reality, which ignores the importance of illusion in the portrayal of reality. Once again, Adorno learnt about illusion from reading Lukács's *History and Class Consciousness*. By illusion, he of course means illusions which have been determined by commodity fetishism. So, here's a second point in which Adorno is turning an idea against Lukács which he first learnt from Lukács. Lukács concentrates too much on narration and not enough on technique, thereby overlooking the subjective nature of his idealised realism, not seeing that a so-called faithful rendering of reality may involve a fuller representation of or a caricature of it, in a way that cuts across Lukács's distinction between the abstract potentialities of modernism and the concrete possibilities of realism.

According to Adorno, all portrayal of subjectivity in a novel, whether solipsistic or not, and however achieved stylistically, is based on illusion which is partly true and partly false. The prevalence of parody in modern art, which Lukács indicts as a major feature of modernist decadence, is due to the recognition by artists of the illusory nature of subjectivity on the part of modern art, which is, according to Adorno, the historical basis of all new art. Far from modern art colluding in extreme subjectivity, Adorno says that if Lukács really looked at the style of these modernist writers, he would see that they're all parodying, criticising, making fun of conventional notions of subjectivity. You may remember that, in the first lecture, I said that one of the things that united the Frankfurt School was their interest in providing a new concept of the subject in relation to traditional philosophy and sociology. Adorno sees this potential in a lot of modern art; where Lukács only sees decadence and mere subjectivity, Adorno sees experiments with subjectivity. Lukács's position also prevents him from distinguishing between different kinds of subjectivity which may be portrayed. Lukács lumps them all together. There's a difference between objectless subjectivity and subjectivity

reconciled with the world by having absorbed the world imagina-
tively into its own confines. In every case, the work takes a critical
posture towards social reality by means of its style, which forms a
mode of subjectivity, not by its content or view of the world.

Therefore, for Adorno, there is no need to choose between Franz
Kafka and Thomas Mann. It's a ridiculous question that Lukács
puts.[18] He scorns the interpretation of Kafka which sees in his writing a vision of 'nothingness' and impotence accomplished by means
of 'realistic symbolism'.[19] Some of you, if you've read some of the
secondary literature on Kafka, may know it's not only Lukács who
interprets Kafka in this way. Instead, in his writings on Kafka – there's
an article on Kafka in *Prisms*, it's on the reading list – Adorno emphasises how Kafka's texts are structured in ways which undermine our
conventional habits of reading, and modes of communicating meaning. For example, he points out, with close reference to and quotation
from Kafka's texts, especially *The Trial* and *The Castle*, how Kafka
frequently pits gestures against dialogue so as to undermine the
intention of the words spoken; how he uses narrative form but
eschews traditional progression in the narrative by substituting various forms of repetition of events, of places, and so on. Kafka thus
produces 'tortuous epics' in which the 'boundary between what is
human and the world of things becomes blurred'.[20] This style – not
content – yields the contours of Kafka's subjectivity. It is an extreme
and absolute subjectivity which does not connect with the external
world – 'objectless inwardness' – which therefore cannot distinguish
itself from the world.[21] Adorno points out that to try and withdraw

---

18   That is, in his essay 'Franz Kafka or Thomas Mann', in Lukács, *The Meaning
of Contemporary Realism*, pp. 47–92.

19   Theodor W. Adorno, 'Notes on Kafka', in *Prisms*, transl. Samuel and Shierry
Weber (Cambridge, MA: MIT Press, 1983), p. 245.

20   Ibid., p. 262.

21   Adorno uses this phrase 'objectless inwardness' in ibid., p. 261. However, he
first developed it to describe Søren Kierkegaard's conception of subjectivity in his
first major work: Theodor W. Adorno, *Kierkegaard: Construction of the Aesthetic*,
transl. Robert Hullot-Kentor (Minneapolis: University of Minnesota Press, 1989).
'Objectless inwardness' is discussed throughout, but see in particular pp. 27–30.

into absolute subjectivity is, strictly speaking, impossible, because words and sentences break any illusion of absolute immediacy, and Kafka's style is designed to avoid this paradox. Secondly, such withdrawal into absolute subjectivity succumbs to the very estrangement of reification which it is trying to escape. Adorno says: 'The subject seeks to break the spell of reification by reifying itself.'[22] That's just the same as what I said about ten or fifteen minutes ago, that certain kinds of radical works, music, and so on, in fact, in their very attempt to escape something of which they are critical, repeat the same disastrous pattern. Another way of putting that is that 'the subject seeks to break the spell of reification by reifying itself'. Adorno, therefore, like Lukács, sees the subjectivity in Kafka's texts, and sees a sense in which the texts collude in the distortion to which they bear witness. However, by focusing on the process of Kafka's style, and the complex contradictions produced in the attempt to express extreme subjectivity, Adorno is able to explain 'terror' and 'isolation' as effects, instead of resorting to them as the ultimate themes of the texts. That's a very important distinction, which will crop up again.

It is the same lack of attention to style which vitiates Lukács's interpretation of Thomas Mann's novels. This is quite funny actually, this story. I don't know if you know it, but I'll tell you. Adorno points out how Lukács tries to explain away Mann's experiments with different perspectives of time in *The Magic Mountain* and in *Doctor Faustus*, and in how he fails to appreciate at all Mann's use of irony as a medium for creating aesthetic distance in his texts – as a way of using and undermining conventional realist illusions in the novel.[23] In fact, as I've said, Lukács didn't even see Mann as a modernist writer, which is really quite incredible. Now the funny thing is that, although Lukács wrote this book on *Doctor Faustus* – I think it's on the reading list – Mann and Adorno had worked together very, very closely on *Doctor Faustus*. Thomas Mann had been particularly impressed by the book by Adorno called *Philosophy of New Music*, which is on your reading

22   Adorno, 'Notes on Kafka', p. 261.
23   Thomas Mann, *The Magic Mountain*, transl. H. T. Lowe-Porter (London: Vintage, 2011).

list, and by another book of Adorno's on Wagner.[24] In letters to Adorno, Mann affirmed his use of what he called 'the principle of montage' in *Doctor Faustus*.[25] It's quite funny because you may remember that Brecht said his works were composed on the principle of montage, too. By this 'principle of montage', Mann meant that he uses precise, naturalistic detail, drawn from a range of sources, precisely to enhance fictional illusion – that you can use naturalistic and realistic detail precisely to create new kinds of illusions so that 'palpable reality was forever indistinguishably merging into painted perspectives and illusions'.[26] He described this as a 'playful' approach – you remember that Lukács describes it as a realistic approach – and endorsed Adorno's criticism of the formal principle of Wagner's work, whereby 'the production [of the work] is hidden by the appearance of the product'.[27] Thomas Mann said to Adorno in letters: when I write a book, unlike conventional literature, I am all the time trying to draw attention to the fact that this is a written book – to the fact that it's been produced by me. I never try to hide the fact that I've written the book. Whereas you may remember that Lukács's notion of realism is based on the very idea that the process of production of the work does not enter into its final form. Mann declared to Adorno: 'The illusory character of the work of art as something real is completely alien to me and has never aroused my ambitions. My relationship to the work was too honourably ironic, and I have always liked humorously compromising the [process of] production.'[28] Thomas Mann is describing his work as playful, ironic, humorous,

---

24   Theodor W. Adorno, *Philosophy of New Music*, transl. Robert Hullot-Kentor (Minneapolis: University of Minnesota Press, 2019); Theodor W. Adorno, *In Search of Wagner*, transl. Rodney Livingstone (London: Verso, 2005).

25   Thomas Mann to Adorno, 30 December 1945, in Theodor W. Adorno and Thomas Mann, *Correspondence: 1943–1955*, ed. Christoph Gödde and Thomas Sprecher, transl. Nicholas Walker (London: Polity, 2006), pp. 11–13.

26   Thomas Mann, *The Story of a Novel: The Genesis of Doctor Faustus*, transl. Richard and Clara Winston (London: Secker & Warburg, 1961), p. 32.

27   Ibid., p. 31; Adorno, *In Search of Wagner*, p. 74, quoted by Mann to Adorno, 30 October 1952, in *Correspondence*, p. 92.

28   Ibid.

and so on. In the light of this, it seems that Lukács has mistakenly taken Mann's novels far too literally, for Mann was not 'in search of bourgeois man' – this is one of Lukács's other articles on Mann – but, in fact, Mann was in search of a style appropriate to modern art as he understood it.[29]

Lukács's interpretation of *Doctor Faustus* is particularly unfortunate. Adorno objects to Lukács's referring to his – that is, Adorno's – own essay on 'The Aging of New Music' in support of Lukács's argument that modern art is decadent.[30] Adorno's point in that essay, and in the book *Philosophy of New Music*, was that new music or modern art is not 'the expression of terror', but a certain stylistic principle which should submit itself to 'insistent self-criticism'.[31] Mann, in fact, based *Doctor Faustus* on Adorno's book *Philosophy of New Music* – it's on your reading list, translated unfortunately as *Philosophy of Modern Music*.[32] Adrian Leverkühn, a central character in *Doctor Faustus*, speaks very large chunks taken from Adorno's book to explain his style of composition, and the music theory expounded by another character in the book, Kretschmar, is also based on Adorno's ideas. That book, *Doctor Faustus*, was really half-written by Adorno. But it is not just music theory but Adorno's whole sociological interpretation of new art which is contained in Mann's book. These ideas are not merely quoted in a way which is restricted to the isolated Leverkühn, whose problems are studied by Mann within the framework of a realist novel, as Lukács said. On the contrary, as Mann explicitly stated, the whole novel is composed on the basis of the

29   See Georg Lukács, 'In Search of Bourgeois Man', in *Essays on Thomas Mann*, pp. 13–46.

30   For Adorno's objection, see 'Extorted Reconciliation', pp. 231–2. For the essay, see Theodor W. Adorno, 'The Aging of New Music', in *Essays on Music*, ed. Richard Leppert (Berkeley: University of California Press, 2002), pp. 181–202.

31   Adorno, 'Extorted Reconciliation', p. 231.

32   The book was originally published in English in 1973 as *Philosophy of Modern Music*, transl. Anne G. Mitchell and Wesley Blomster (New York: Seabury). Subsequently the book has been re-translated by Robert Hullot-Kentor, and published as *Philosophy of New Music* (Minneapolis: University of Minnesota Press, 2019).

same principles and contradictions which structure the possibility of style in new music: 'to portray the whole cultural crisis in addition to the crisis of music was the fundamental motif of my book . . . I felt clearly that the book itself would have to become the thing it dealt with: . . . constructivist music.'[33] In fact, if Lukács had realised this, Lukács would have to have condemned the whole of Mann's work. Do you remember, Lukács said that Mann had written a realist book? That Leverkühn was there in his study, suffering, producing this contradictory art, and the commentator was outside, identified in space and time, and making a sort of sociological commentary on this isolated, decadent, corrupt artist? That was the definition, for Lukács, of a realist novel. In fact, Thomas Mann himself was deeply influenced by Adorno's ideas, as a result of which Thomas Mann himself said that the whole book – and of course you can't isolate Leverkühn and the commentator, who's just as much a modernist experiment as Leverkühn in his study – Thomas Mann said that the whole book is an experiment with the possibility of new style in both art and music; and therefore, the only consistent position for Lukács to take would have been to have said that the whole book is decadent. Since Lukács didn't understand what the book was about, he didn't say that. We've particularly caught Lukács out here, because he's given his realist interpretation of a book which was largely written by Adorno.[34]

I've got a couple of concluding points. I'd just like to pull together the way in which Adorno's criticisms of Lukács, Brecht, and Sartre – I know we haven't discussed Sartre, but we have discussed Lukács and Brecht – are all based on the same argument. I'd just like to summarise what that argument is. Adorno has sought to demonstrate that Brecht's attempt in drama to avoid representation of subjectivity is as self-contradictory as Kafka's attempt to withdraw into absolute subjectivity. Adorno criticises Sartre's dramaturgy on the same grounds as he criticises Brecht's: for demanding a changed attitude, instead of compelling it; although Sartre's demand is, of course, quite

---

33   Mann, *Story of a Novel*, pp. 54–5.
34   This is a playful overstatement.

different from Brecht's.[35] (I hope you sort of remember that last lecture on Brecht, because I'm picking up some themes that came up there.) What Adorno is opposed to in all these cases – in the case of Lukács, in the case of Kafka, in the case of Brecht, in the case of Sartre – is what I call 'artistic and literary thematics' – that is, to composing or understanding works of art according to interpretations of their ostensible themes. He is equally critical of Lukács's reading of modernist style according to existential themes, as he is of Brecht's composing of plays in the cause of political themes, as he is of Sartre's composing of plays according to explicit existential themes. These explicit commitments tend to restructure meaning or style in a way which reinstates precisely what the theme tends to eliminate – usually some form of subjectivity. For example, the theme of Sartre's plays is the absurdity and meaninglessness of existence. But, to make this theme into the clear message of his plays is to confer on it a positive meaning, and thereby to contradict its own intention. The mistake, common to Sartre and Brecht, is that they try to destroy the autonomy of artistic meaning – that is, they try to avoid the fact that meaning in literature is based on the illusion that a literal, ordinary word, once used in a fictional text, retains its literal meaning entirely. They seek to renounce the changing meaning which occurs once words are, as it were, transcribed into a work of art. But, because they do not concede the necessity of illusion, they therefore assimilate themselves to that illusion, instead of arming themselves against whatever power gives verisimilitude to that illusion.

Now I just want to say a couple of things to sum this up. You might think, if you go back to the beginning of this course, that this is rather funny. You might think that a Marxist or a sociological literary theory would be precisely interested in the content or the themes of works of art – that that's where you'd find social content – wouldn't you? Would you? Would you have done originally? What I've argued for is the position – and I think that it is a radically sociological position – that you cannot assess something's political or social importance by trying

35 See especially Theodor W. Adorno, 'Commitment', in *Notes to Literature*, vol. 2, pp. 76–94.

to read off its social content, or – where Benjamin or Brecht is concerned – by trying to give it an explicit political or social content. We've got here a position which claims to be radically Marxist or sociological, which is saying that you don't give a Marxist or sociological interpretation of art by reading off social content or social themes. You must look at style, or technical features of a work of art. That's not as asociological as it might sound, because it's based on this generalising of Marx's theory of commodity fetishism. It's based on a theory which says that we live in a society in which some things which seem to be comprehensible to us are not really, and some things which seem to be incomprehensible to us are really comprehensible. This applies just as much to all those social institutions which commodity fetishism effects as it does to works of art. Adorno tries to connect commodity fetishism in society at large with its reoccurrence in works of art.

I intend to stop there. I would like it now – if some of you want to stay; if some of you don't, you could go – if we could relax a bit and draw together and talk more intimately.

Afterword
Martin Jay

Gillian Rose was in many ways a unique figure, whose rapidly evolving intellectual journey became publicly intertwined with the dramatic closing events of her abbreviated life.[1] Not only did she have the courage to tackle the thorniest of philosophical, theological, and social issues, but in her defiant struggle with a fatal illness and wager on the consolations of love and faith, she also showed that philosophy could combine a search for the truth with the quest for a meaningful life.[2] Apparently abstract considerations of the convoluted relationships between law and violence, reason and belief, the individual and the community, were imbued with existential significance. Although the full impact of her example could not be

---

1   Andrew Brower Latz has compiled a thorough bibliography, not only of her work, but also of the many reactions to it during and after her life: 'Gillian Rose Bibliography', at academia.edu. His later *The Social Philosophy of Gillian Rose* (Eugene, OR: Cascade, 2018) should be added to the list. My own speculations about how her life and work might have been related can be found in 'The Conversion of the Rose', *Refractions of Violence* (New York: Routledge, 2003).

2   Pierre Hadot, *Philosophy as a Way of Life*, ed. Arnold Davidson, transl. Michael Chase (Malden, MA: Wiley-Blackwell, 1995); Mathew Sharpe and Michael Ure, *Philosophy as a Way of Life: History, Dimensions, Directions* (London: Bloomsbury, 2021).

appreciated until her life neared its premature end, it was clear from the beginning of Gillian Rose's career that her scholarly work was invested with the passion and commitment of someone who understood philosophy as far more than a bloodless exercise in logic-chopping or argumentation for its own sake.[3]

The lecture series Rose gave to the 'Modern European Mind' undergraduates at the University of Sussex in the winter of 1979 grew out of her early interest in the Frankfurt School, Theodor W. Adorno in particular. The previous year, she had published her first book, *The Melancholy Science,* based on a dissertation written at Oxford under the wary supervision of the émigré Polish philosopher Leszek Kołakowski, who had long since abandoned his early Marxist humanist sympathies.[4] Although subtitled *An Introduction to the Thought of Theodor W. Adorno*, it was an ambitious and uncompromising reckoning with Adorno's legacy rather than a text for beginners. In it, she stressed the inextricability of Adorno's writing style and the content of his thought, provocatively interpreted his idiosyncratic understanding of reification, and defended him against the assumption that, because his *Wissenschaft* was *traurige*, he was a resigned and pessimistic quietist.

Although by and large a defence of the current relevance of Adorno's work, *The Melancholy Science* also contained hints of Rose's later turn away from his negative dialectics to Hegel's more positive alternative. Walter Benjamin's influence on Adorno was by and large blamed for his deficiencies:

> The most apparently 'Hegelian' aspects of Adorno's materialism, such as his concern with the 'concrete' and with 'identity' were always too imbued with Benjamin's ideas to make sense from a

---

3 Rose, to be sure, sought to eradicate the residues of subjectivity in idealism, and fought the psychologistic reduction of ideas to the lived experience of those who generated them. In the lectures, this attitude is demonstrated, for example, in her attack on Hannah Arendt for introducing 'the infuriating stress on the personal aspects of Benjamin's life' (p. 72).

4 Gillian Rose, *The Melancholy Science: An Introduction to the Thought of Theodor W. Adorno* (London: Verso, 2014).

Hegelian perspective. Missing from Adorno's work is the Hegelian notion of 'self-reference'; missing from the Marxism of both men is any notion of human activity or praxis.[5]

Rose's desire to rescue Adorno from Benjamin was evident in the excoriating review she published in 1979 of Susan Buck-Morss's *The Origin of Negative Dialectics*, which she claimed had exaggerated his continuing debts to Benjamin's anti-Hegelian impulses in his later work.[6] Although arguing that Adorno should not be simply classified as a Hegelian Marxist, she was not yet ready to consider this a deficiency fatal to his thought.

By the time *Hegel Contra Sociology* was published in 1981, however, Rose had given up her attempt to rescue Adorno from Benjamin, and now included him along with virtually every other modern thinker in the camp of neo-Kantians deaf to the still potent insights of Hegel's philosophy. Despite Adorno's frequent criticisms of Kant and his fully warranted objection to Lukács's solution to the antinomies of bourgeois thought because of its Fichtean subjectivism, he himself had failed in two major respects. First, he had been too quick to jettison a positive philosophy of historical redemption: 'Adorno's rejection of all philosophy of history, all teleologies of reconciliation, whether Hegelian, Marxist or Lukácsian, meant that he could not underpin his analyses of cultural forms with analysis of those economic forms on which the cogency of the theory of commodity fetishism depends.'[7] And, second, he had fallen back on a 'morality of method' in which the problematic separation of dialectical method from dialectical substance – a distinction forthrightly urged by Lukács – was inadvertently duplicated: 'Paradoxically, Adorno's thought

5   Ibid., p. 37.

6   Gillian Rose, review of Susan Buck-Morss, 'Review: *The Origin of Negative Dialectics*, by Theodor W. Adorno, Walter Benjamin and the Frankfurt Institute, and *The Frankfurt School: The Critical Theory of Max Horkheimer and Theodor W. Adorno*, by Zoltán Tar', *History and Theory* 18: 1 (1979), p. 126–35. Rose was no less critical of the second book, which she also accused of failing to understand the importance of Adorno's style and over-emphasising his biography.

7   Gillian Rose, *Hegel Contra Sociology* (London: Verso, 1981), p. 32.

becomes methodological too. For he developed a Nietzschean "morality of method" in the place of the discredited philosophies of history, and this represents a return to neo-Kantianism on his part.'[8] Whereas, in *The Melancholy Science,* Rose had lauded Nietzsche's positive influence on Adorno's style, now she ruefully concluded that his thought 'has some affinities with some versions of academic neo-Kantianism'.[9] For the rest of her career, Rose would lament what she would call in a 1987 lecture Adorno's retreat from 'speculative' to 'dialectical' thinking, by which she meant a negative dialectics valorising non-identity over reconciliation.[10]

By so defiantly embracing an uncompromising version of speculative idealism, insisting that reason and ethical truth were, despite all, immanent in reality, Rose was blazing a path in late-twentieth-century philosophy that few would follow. Her call to embrace 'inaugurated mourning', drawing on the healing power of forgiveness to overcome the endless 'aberrated mourning' or saturnine melancholy

---

8   Georg Lukács, *History and Class Consciousness: Studies in Marxist Dialectics,* transl. Rodney Livingstone (Cambridge, MA: Harvard University Press, 1971). After conceding that all of Marx's individual theses might be disproved, he defiantly asserted that 'orthodox Marxism' did not 'imply the uncritical acceptance of the results of Marx's investigations. It is not the "belief" in this or that thesis, nor the exegesis of a "sacred" book. On the contrary, orthodoxy refers exclusively to *method*' (p. 1 – emphasis in original). In one of the few commentaries on Rose's early work, Tony Gorman argues that she also 'holds to Lukács's tenet that Marxism is a "method" of philosophising rather than a fixed doctrine'. Tony Gorman, 'Gillian Rose and the Project of a Critical Marxism', *Radical Philosophy* 105 (January–February 2001), pp. 25, 33. Without ever considering speculative philosophy a 'fixed doctrine', she nonetheless came to reject the distinction between method and substance as a residue of neo-Kantian antinomial thinking. For Gorman's reflections on Rose's later development, see his 'Gillian Rose and the Critique of Violence', *Radical Philosophy* 197 (May–June 2016), p. 33. For a defence of Adorno against this charge, see Simon Jarvis, *Adorno: A Critical Introduction* (Cambridge: Polity, 1998), p. 52.

9   Ibid.

10   Gillian Rose, 'From Speculative to Dialectical Thinking: From Hegel to Adorno', in *Judaism and Modernity: Philosophical Essays* (London: Verso, 1993). The essay was first delivered at a conference at UCLA on 'The Frankfurt School Today', in 1987.

she lamented in Walter Benjamin, was not widely heeded.[11] Her later explorations of the political-theological legacies of Jewish and Christian thought and fierce denunciation of the postmodernist celebration of otherness and difference would move her still further away from her initial enthusiasm for Western Marxism in general and the Frankfurt School, with its stress on the value of non-identity, in particular.

Rose's lectures on 'Marxist Modernism' take us back to an earlier period when she was first absorbing and responding with enthusiasm to the still unfolding legacy of Critical Theory. They were, let it be admitted, clearly not intended to be preserved for posterity. As is often the case with the posthumous publication of the transcripts of a prominent intellectual's talks, their appearing in print may, in fact, risk being seen as an unintended betrayal. In this particular case, not only are they pitched at a more conversational and informal level than Rose's written work, which always hovered at the highest altitude of complexity, but they also contain a number of factual slips that would have doubtless been caught in the vetting process of a manuscript submitted to a scholarly press.[12] A thinker careful about

---

11   Gillian Rose, 'Walter Benjamin – Out of the Sources of Modern Judaism', in *Judaism and Modernity*, p. 209.

12   For the record: the Second International was more than an annual meeting, as it had a permanent executive after 1900 called the International Socialist Bureau; Horkheimer became director of the Institut für Sozialforschung in 1930, not 1929; Ernst Bloch was not a composer (Rose may have been confusing him with Ernest Bloch); Bloch did not 'escape Stalinism', but after the war returned to it, leaving East Germany only after the building of the Wall in 1961; Bloch was never close to Thomas Mann, and was not an editor of *Mass und Wert*, the journal Mann co-edited with Konrad Falke; Benjamin's *One-Way Street*, published in 1928, was not a 'discussion of living in Berlin during the Depression of the late 1920s'; Benjamin's dialectical images were not 'social types'; Benjamin was never in a 'Nazi concentration camp', but rather in the French work camp Clos Saint-Joseph, near Nevers; Benjamin did not publish his 'Theses on the Philosophy of History' before his suicide; Brecht did not reject Benjamin's 'Work of Art' essay for *Das Wort* – another of its editors, Willi Bredel, did; existentialism did not typically endorse the idea that 'the unity of consciousness is the basis of all reality'; socialist realism was not 'to the left' of *Proletkult*, nor was it developed jointly by Lukács and Stalin (Maxim Gorky's 1934 speech was a turning point, and there were many antecedents in the previous decade).

the nuances of her ideas and fastidious about the ways in which they are expressed might be additionally chagrined if the unpublished material expresses early opinions that were later repudiated.

And yet, outweighing the risk of contravening the likely reluctance of their author is the benefit of revealing the intellectual journey that culminated in her mature work. Rather than a betrayal, their publication expresses, we might say, the admiring judgement of posterity that even the seemingly ephemeral remnants of the life of this particular mind are worth preserving, and, indeed, may still have something to teach us. Or, in the Hegelian terms Rose would have appreciated, they can be seen as moments in a dialectical process where there are no errors to be regretted, only aspects of partial truth that are incorporated into the whole. Whether or not this vindication is persuasive, the lectures justify publication on their own merit. They document Rose's early desire to educate students in the virtues of a Critical Theory that had emerged in the context of aesthetic modernism in the early twentieth century. Here, it was enough to spell out the need for a revitalised Marxism that would meet the challenges of a still unjust capitalist system that has devised new ways of occluding its contradictions and fending off a terminal crisis. In this effort, however, the lectures also reveal something of Rose's eccentric role in the general reception of Western Marxism, indeed continental theory in general, during the late 1970s in the Anglophone world.

To address the latter first, it is striking that nowhere is the name Louis Althusser mentioned. Ever since the translation of *For Marx* in 1969, Althusser was a figure to conjure with, especially on the British Left, or at least that portion of it open to theoretical ideas from across the Channel. One of the most explosive episodes of that era was the polemic launched by E. P. Thompson's Marxist humanist attack on Althusserianism in *The Poverty of Theory* in 1978, which was countered by Perry Anderson a short time later in *Arguments within English Marxism*.[13] Rose, however, was entirely outside this debate,

---

13   E. P. Thompson, *The Poverty of Theory and Other Essays* (London: Merlin, 1978); Perry Anderson, *Arguments within English Marxism* (London: NLB, 1980). The dispute continues to reverberate. For a recent consideration, see Christian Fuchs,

which, since the mid 1960s, had pitted an older generation of British leftists against the younger generation around the *New Left Review.*[14] She did not appear in its pages, and only deigned to consider Althusser in passing in a 'note' in *Hegel Contra Sociology*, where he is derided as 'unique in making all the classic neo-Kantian moves within a project of re-reading Marx'.[15] Thompson's mixture of exhaustive empirical research and humanist stress on subjective rather than structural factors did not merit her attention at all. After a quick nod to existentialists like Sartre, and without any mention at all of Gramsci, Rose focused entirely on German rather than French, Italian, or British Marxists, with the Hungarian Georg Lukács included as an honorary member of the Teutonic cohort. There was enough to do, she reasoned, in explaining their ideas in the contexts of the rapidly changing role of Marxism in the wake of the Bolshevik Revolution and the failure of its central European counterparts, along with contemporaneous developments in aesthetic modernism.

What is perhaps even more noteworthy are the implicit tensions in the lectures with the arguments Rose made elsewhere around the same time. Rather than bemoaning, as she did in *The Melancholy Science*, Benjamin's anti-Hegelian influence on Adorno, she tried to rescue him instead for Marxism against those who would read him as primarily a theological thinker.[16] She also accepted, without apparent qualification, the value of a sociological approach to cultural and

---

'Revisiting the Althusser/E. P. Thompson Controversy: Toward a Marxist Theory of Communication', *Communication and the Public* 4: 1 (2019), pp. 3–20. As far as I can tell, Rose never engaged with Thompson.

14   See Abe Walker, 'Theory, History and Methodological Positivism in the Anderson–Thompson Debate', *Formations* 1: 1 (2010), p. 13–29.

15   Rose, *Hegel Contra Sociology*, p. 37.

16   Perhaps the most prominent Anglophone advocate at the time of saving Benjamin for the Marxist camp was Terry Eagleton. See his *Walter Benjamin: Or, Towards a Revolutionary Criticism* (London: Verso, 1981). In Germany, the defenders of a stubbornly Marxist reading of Benjamin were critical of the ways Adorno and Gershom Scholem had allegedly edited his work in order to diminish its militancy. Some even contended that Horkheimer and the Institute had been ambivalent about fully supporting him during his Paris exile, and were not genuinely committed to rescuing him from Europe.

aesthetic issues. In the helpful glossary affixed to *The Melancholy Science*, Rose had noted that, although he may have titled his books 'the philosophy of . . .' or 'the sociology of . . .', 'In each case Adorno is referring to his own enterprise which is always the same. He is usually guided by the predominance of the discipline which he is criticising: he calls his own work "philosophy" when he is criticising philosophy, and "sociology" when he is criticising sociology.'[17] Only a few years later, however, she would argue more intransigently that 'the very idea of a scientific sociology, whether non-Marxist or Marxist, is only possible as a form of neo-Kantianism'.[18]

And yet, in these lectures, Rose can still tell her students with apparent approval that 'Adorno developed a systematic Marxist sociology of art' (p. 108), and that Benjamin 'developed a sociology of the relationship between art forms and different kinds of societies' (p. 64).[19] Nor does she formulate a distinction between Bloch's idiosyncratic utopian theorising and the discipline of sociology. The basis for these assertions is the claim that they were all generalising from Lukács's expansive reading of Marx's analysis of commodity fetishism, understood as the transformation of relations between humans into phantasmagoric ones between things.[20] Interestingly, Rose argues

17   Rose, *Melancholy Science*, p. 152.

18   Rose, *Hegel Contra Sociology*, pp. 1–2. Her argument against sociology echoes Lukács's critique in the 1920s of Nikolai Bukharin's sociological interpretation of historical materialism. See his *Tactics and Ethics: Political Writings, 1919–1929*, ed. Michael McColgan, transl. Rodney Livingstone (London: Verso, 1972), pp. 134–42.

19   Rose's 1976 dissertation had in fact been titled, 'Reification as a Sociological Category: Theodor W. Adorno's Concept of Reification and the Possibility of a Critical Theory of Society'. In these lectures, she asserts that 'Benjamin's work was radical and sociological before he was influenced by Marxism' (p. 55), showing her still positive appreciation of sociology, while exaggerating Benjamin's debts to that discipline.

20   In *The Melancholy Science*, Rose noted that the traditional English translation of the passage from Marx's *Capital* as 'the fantastic form of a relation between men' should have been 'the phantasmagoric form', which drew on the idea of a 'crowd or succession of dim or doubtfully real persons' (p. 31). She argued that Benjamin and Adorno had picked up on the importance of phantasmagorias in their analysis of modern capitalist experience. In *Hegel Contra Sociology*, she could still approvingly call the theory of commodity fetishism 'the most speculative moment in Marx's exposition of capital' (p. 217).

that Adorno was the most consistent of all of them in applying Marx's theory of commodity fetishism 'to every stage of production, exchange, distribution and reception of artworks' (p. 107). He sought to demonstrate, 'as any good sociologist would' (p. 110), that the abstraction engendered by that process meant that what seemed subjectively determined was in fact determined by objective social forces. If Adorno thought there is contradiction that develops in the artistic sphere, Rose tells her students, it is between the forces of production of artworks and their relations of exchange, between increasingly esoteric creations of isolated 'high' or 'avant-garde' artists and the exchange of commodities in what he and Max Horkheimer would later call 'the culture industry'.

Adopting Marx's analysis of commodity fetishism and the distinction between use and exchange value meant for Rose that the Frankfurt School was liberated from the reductive metaphor of base and superstructure that had hampered earlier Marxist attempts to understand culture. It also meant that they were less focused on the role of alienated labour in capitalism than the 'humanist' Marxists who were enamoured of his 1844 manuscripts. Nor did they fall prey to the fallacy that reification – a term Marx himself had never used – was essentially a subjective, psychological, or ideological error that could be corrected by a change of consciousness alone. But the conclusions, political, cultural, and historical, they drew from their stress on commodity fetishism – and this is one of Rose's primary insights – were by no means identical. Recruiting arguments derived from theorists like Nietzsche and Freud, who were outside the Marxist tradition narrowly construed, they came up with a variety of suggestive positions, which in a way paralleled the experiments in literary, visual, and musical form being carried out at the same time by aesthetic modernists.

Rose's exploration of the dynamic interaction between Western Marxist theory and modernist art was very much at the cutting edge of leftist theoretical discussion in the 1970s. Following Fredric Jameson's seminal *Marxism and Form*, which appeared in 1971, interest had quickened in the complex historical relationship between the two avant-gardes, political and aesthetic, and in the ways in which

Western Marxism might illuminate current cultural struggles.[21] A year or so before Rose's lectures, New Left Books published a selection of essential texts by Lukács, Bloch, Adorno, Benjamin, and Brecht under the title *Aesthetics and Politics*.[22] Although a thorough consideration of their relations to modernist aesthetics had to await Eugene Lunn's *Marxism and Modernism* in 1984, Rose's lectures helpfully distinguish which variant of modernist aesthetics each found palatable or not.[23] One of her criticisms of Lukács's defence of realism is against its lumping together of all varieties of modernism – expressionism, cubism, surrealism, dada, as well as individual figures such as Kafka, Joyce, and Proust, who were outside of movements – as if they were inherently equivalent. This led to his tendentious equations of modernism with irrationalism and irrationalism with fascism, which earned her justified ire. She lodges another complaint against Lukács's complacent assumption that a socialist version of realism was possible because socialism was already being realised in the Soviet Union.

Rose, however, is also careful to distance herself from some of the assumptions her other protagonists held concerning the critical implications of the modernist art they championed. Thus, for example, she takes Bloch to task for his hasty belief that the desire of modernist artists, expressionists in particular, was to produce works that genuinely transcend their society. Mediated as they are by the commodification of all relations in capitalism, even the most unconventional artworks cannot entirely escape the gravitational pull of the status quo. Nor was Bloch right in attributing universal implications to subjective emotion, which was more likely an expression of a

---

21   Fredric Jameson, *Marxism and Form: Twentieth-Century Dialectical Theories of Literature* (Princeton, NJ: Princeton University Press, 1971).

22   Ernst Bloch, Georg Lukács, Bertolt Brecht, Walter Benjamin, and Theodor W. Adorno, *Aesthetics and Politics*, afterword by Fredric Jameson (London: NLB, 1977).

23   Eugene Lunn, *Marxism and Modernism: An Historical Study of Lukács, Brecht, Benjamin and Adorno* (Berkeley, CA: University of California Press, 1984). In one of those sad coincidences that mean nothing but are nonetheless sobering, both Lunn and Rose died of cancer at the age of forty-eight.

Afterword

139

specific historical situation than anything beyond it. And, finally, he shared with Lukács an apocalyptic vision of bourgeois culture in the throes of its collapse, which Rose argued was prematurely optimistic about its terminal crisis (as were more economically focused Marxists who banked on the internal contradictions of 'late capitalism').

Rose's lecture on Benjamin shows her uncertain grappling with his legacy (which, to be fair, was still only very imperfectly understood in the 1970s). For example, although she is right to note the crucial importance of his concept of experience, which was directed against its empirical version, she mistakenly identifies it with the traditional German notion of *Bildung* or humanist self-formation, which in fact became one of his targets.[24] If, as she points out, Benjamin took seriously *Proletkult* aesthetic experiments, she might have noted that they were based on a very different pedagogical model than that embraced by the *Bildungsbürgertum* he so despised.[25] Rose also labels such texts as *Berlin Childhood around 1900* and *One-Way Street* 'sociological autobiographies', which fails to register their challenge to the conventions of both sociology and autobiography.[26] Another of her claims, that Benjamin believed in original sin but interpreted it as meaning the sins of social democracy, may be ingenious, but is not

24   During Benjamin's early involvement with the Jewish youth movement, he was influenced by the ideology of *Bildung*; but, like many other radical Jews in the interwar era, he abandoned it. See Steven E. Aschheim, 'German Jews beyond *Bildung* and Liberalism: The Radical Jewish Revival in the Weimar Republic', in *Culture and Catastrophe: German and Jewish Confrontations with National Socialism and Other Crises* (New York: NYU Press, 1996).

25   See, for example, his 'Program for a Children's Proletarian Theater' (1928 or 1929), in *Walter Benjamin: Selected Writings*, vol. 2, part 1, *1927–1930*, ed. Michael W. Jennings, Howard Eiland and Gary Smith, transl. Rodney Livingstone and others (Cambridge, MA: Belknap, 1999), which shows the influence of his Latvian lover Asja Lacis in calling for class conscious education and the liberation of children's collaborative imagination. In contrast, he writes, 'Youth Culture attempts to achieve a hopeless compromise: it drains the enthusiasm of young people by a process of idealistic self-reflection, so as gradually and imperceptibly to replace the formal ideologies of German idealism by the contents of the bourgeois class' (p. 205).

26   See Gerhard Richter, *Walter Benjamin and the Corpus of Autobiography* (Detroit, MI: Wayne State University Press, 2002).

ultimately convincing.[27] Rose also posits Benjamin's alleged affinity for parody, a genre he never seriously promoted, and bizarrely asserts that Benjamin forgot that the 'masses are not yet victorious'. And yet, despite all of these lapses, her lecture on Benjamin ends with the important insight that his ambivalences alert us to the ways in which aesthetic modernism, *pace* Lukács, was a contested field with as many progressive as regressive impulses.

Ambivalences – or, more accurately, the nuances of negative dialectics – are more sensitively registered in her concise but trenchant account of Horkheimer and Adorno's *Dialectic of Enlightenment*. In addition to dispelling misconceptions of the book – for example, that it was an unqualified elitist defence of all avant-garde culture against its popular alternative – Rose also provides several insights about its provocative argument that retain their power. She makes a case for the importance of Nietzsche's critique of rationality in moving Horkheimer and Adorno beyond a Marxist class analysis of fascism and the liberal *Sonderweg* (special path) theory that blames it on Germany's particular departure from a normative notion of Western modernisation. She stresses the structural function of anti-Semitism – the concealment of domination in economic production – rather than its psychological dimension in their explanation of the over-determined hatred of the Jews. And she notes the still audacious implications of their conclusion that the potential for a revival of fascism remains alarmingly strong even in the democratic West, which also reflected the empirical conclusions of their parallel study, *The Authoritarian Personality*.

In her discussion of the Frankfurt School's analysis of the Culture Industry, which is one of the high points of her lectures, Rose suggestively identifies both creative composition – the development of original aesthetic techniques – and the pseudo-individualist

---

27   For a careful reconstruction of the complexities of Benjamin's thoughts on original sin, see Eric Jacobson, *Metaphysics of the Profane: The Political Theology of Walter Benjamin and Gershom Scholem* (New York: Columbia University Press, 2003), Chapter 5. Benjamin, to be sure, did disdain the evolutionary gradualism of revisionist social democracy, but not because it was evidence of sinfulness, original or otherwise.

standardisation of commercial forms of entertainment as variants of the forces of production that traditional Marxists had understood in terms of the technological underpinnings of economic modes. Rather than holding out hope for technological change as the engine of emancipation in the spirit of Benjamin and Brecht, Horkheimer and Adorno worried that it only increased the power of the second type of productive force at the expense of the first. Drawing on Adorno's analysis of musical developments, Rose illustrates the change by juxtaposing the dwindling ability to listen to classical music as an intelligible totality, often based on themes with variations, with the mind-numbing repetition of standardised motifs in popular music.[28] In other words, the abstract exchange principle that rules what Marxists call the relations of production has also come to character-ise the forces of production in the sphere of culture. Only certain esoteric artistic creations escape its gravitational pull, although at the cost of losing any meaningful reception by a mass audience, whose capacity to listen intelligently has regressed.

But even the most avant-garde art can serve dubious ends. In her lecture on Brecht, she skilfully connects the dots between his (and Benjamin's) critique of certain modernist movements, the *Neue Sachlichkeit* in particular, and Herbert Marcuse's later critiques of 'repressive tolerance' and 'repressive desublimation'. Although glid-ing a bit too quickly over the differences between creating non-political modern art, tolerating reactionary ideas, and promoting direct libidinal satisfaction in a still unfree society, she alerts her

---

28   Adorno's idea of the regression of listening skills may on the surface seem like an expression of his snobbery or elitism. But a deliberate learning process did take place when classical music, liberated from its devotional function, gained an audience among the educated middle classes in Europe, which receded in subsequent years. Richard Taruskin, who was in fact one of Adorno's most unforgiving critics, noted the importance of Haydn in particular in this process. See his 'Haydn and the Enlightenment?', in *Cursed Questions: On Music and Its Social Practices* (Berkeley: University of California Press, 2020). The ability to listen intelligently is, we would now be more inclined than Adorno to acknowledge, culturally determined. However well trained a Western ear might be, it is unlikely to follow, say, the formal complexities of an Indian raga.

listeners to the ways in which even the most apparently critical intentions can be thwarted by a system capable of incorporating virtually all transgressive energies. She goes so far as to attribute to Adorno the conclusion 'that the modernist position is as inherently self-defeating, and is as full of self-contradictions, as any popular music or art' (p. 116).

Included in this judgement, she tells us, is Adorno's sombre claim that Brecht's own 'epic theatre' was, despite all his best efforts, a victim of the same process. He was critical, and with reason according to Rose, of Brecht's didactic experiments because of their reliance on militant content, or what she calls 'artistic and literary thematics' rather than formal innovation, as well as their tacit instrumentalisation of reason for political purposes. Generalising this lesson, Rose cautions her students that 'many forms of radical activity – whether artistic, political, social, theoretical – are fated to display "the same disastrous pattern" which they seek to combat' (p. 114). And yet, her final lecture does allow some glimmer of hope for resistance to the complete recuperation of negation by the totality of late capitalism, which she locates in stylistic and formal innovations that foreshadow a renewal of unreified subjectivity. Kafka is her chief example in literary terms, but, against Lukács's reading of Thomas Mann as a realist, she also spies them in his work, while stressing his debt to Adorno in writing *Doctor Faustus*.

Reading these lectures more than four decades after they were delivered, and with the knowledge we now have of the ongoing reception and subsequent history of Critical Theory – as well as Gillian Rose's own evolution away from many of their arguments – is an unsettling experience. It is moving to hear her informal voice attempting to convey to undergraduates the excitement she felt at rediscovering a tradition of radical thought that seemed increasingly relevant at the time she was lecturing. Her judgements were still fluid enough about which aspects of that tradition should profitably be developed to prevent her from adopting the severe, at times imperious tone that would characterise her later crusade against neo-Kantian sociology in the name of the Hegelian absolute. There is no hint of the turn towards the theological conundrums and existential struggles that would inform her 'secular faith'.[29] The young Rose favoured critical over speculative reason, outrage at social injustice over affirming the unending dialectic of law and violence, the promise of a different future contained in aesthetic form over believing that eternity exists in the here and now for those with faith. This is a Gillian Rose still bridling against the costs of 'the broken middle' rather than sublating them through a synthesis combining the legacies of Athens and Jerusalem. There is no doubt that the mature Gillian Rose would have considered these lectures the efforts of a naive, perhaps even jejune thinker, who had yet to pass through the life-altering experiences that would result in her being able, despite everything, to affirm the work of love. For those who prefer a 'melancholy science', with all of its negative energy, to the consolations of a world where 'mourning becomes the law', they may, however, still have much to teach us.

---

29   See Vincent Lloyd, 'The Secular Faith of Gillian Rose', *Journal of Religious Ethics* 36: 4 (2008).

Index